The Many Deaths
of Danny Rosales

and other plays

Carlos Morton

Arte Público Press
Houston
1983

Acknowledgements

The following plays were published as works in progress: "Las Many Muertes de Richard Morales" in *Conjunto*, "El Jardín" in *El grito*, "Los Dorados" in *Metamorfosis* and "Rancho Hollywood" in *Revista Chicano-Riqueña*. They have all been revised for publication in this collection.

This project is made possible through a grant from the Texas Commission on the Arts.

Arte Público Press
Revista Chicano-Riqueña
University of Houston
Houston, Texas 77004

Library of Congress Catalog No. 82-072277   ISBN 0-934770-16-6

Second Printing: 1987

Printed in the United States of America

To the memory of my father, Staff Sergeant Siro Morton (Retired).

With Special Thanks To:

Dr. Jorge Huerta
Carmen Zapata and the Bilingual Foundation of the Arts
San Francisco Mime Troupe
El Teatro Bilingüe de Houston
San Diego On Stage
The Second City

CONTENTS

The Many Deaths of Danny Rosales

Las Many Muertes de Danny Rosales *was developed in association with and produced by the Bilingual Foundation of the Arts in August 1980.*

CHARACTERS

ROWENA SALDIVAR
BAILIFF
JUDGE
HAROLD PEARL
BERTA ROSALES
STEVE PETERS

FRED HALL
DANNY ROSALES
KIKI VENTURA
GRACE HALL
DEBBIE HALL
DEPUTY BILLY JOE DAVIS

SCENE

In and around Arroyo County, Texas, 1975.

ACT I

ROWENA: In September 1975, on a moonlit gravel road five miles west of town, Fred Hall, the 52-year-old police chief, put the barrel of a 12-gauge sawed-off shotgun under the left armpit of Danny Rosales and pulled the trigger. *(Behind scrim, in silhouette, we see Hall struggle with Rosales. Rosales falls, a shot is heard.)*

BAILIFF: *(Voice, offstage.)* All rise! Court is now in session!

JUDGE: *(Voice, from above.)* Good morning, we are here to arraign Fred Hall, you may be seated.

HAROLD: Your Honor, my client, Fred Hall, is too ill to appear today for the arraignment proceedings. He is suffering from a chronic brain syndrome and neurosurgery is seriously being considered.

BERTA: *(At Rowena's side.)* Rowena, what is he talking about? I saw the sheriff and his wife grocery shopping in Dallas just two days ago.

ROWENA: He is trying to make the sheriff out to be crazy, Berta, that way he can be found not guilty by reason of insanity.

HAROLD: Your Honor, I move that a sanity hearing be set. I propose to call several witnesses who will testify that my client is not mentally competent to stand trial.

ROWENA: Your Honor, I object to any further postponement of this trial. It has already been nine months since Danny Rosales' death.

JUDGE: Miss Saldivar, I hear tell that you are a recent graduate of the Harvard University Law School, are you not?

ROWENA: Yes, I am, your Honor, but I don't see what . . .

JUDGE: Please bear with us, Miss Saldivar. We here in Texas move at a more leisurely pace than you do up north. But that doesn't mean we are not sticklers for detail. Remember that it is the object of the court to insure that the accused receives a fair trial. Your objection is overruled. A sanity hearing will be set for May 24. Mr. Pearl, will you approach the bench? *(As they talk silently.)*

BERTA: Rowena, why are they dragging it out so long?

ROWENA: It's just another tactic on the part of the defense.

BERTA: What does that mean?

ROWENA: He's just trying to buy some more time for his client. But don't worry, we'll find Fred Hall sane enough to stand trial.

HAROLD: Your Honor, I further move for a change of venue from Arroyo County to Jim Bowie County on the grounds that biased publicity has made it impossible for my client to receive a fair trial here.

BERTA: What's he saying now, Rowena?

ROWENA: He is trying to have the trial changed from this county, where there is a high percentage of Mexican American voters, to another county where there are none.

BERTA: No entiendo, explícamelo.

ROWENA: This means, if he gets his way, there won't be any Chicanos on the jury. *(To the judge.)* Your Honor, is the defense implying that Fred Hall cannot receive a fair trial in your court?

HAROLD: I am implying no such thing. My motion is based on evidence gathered from this radical Chicano newspaper which pictures my client as a pig and an ogre. There is a climate of racial hatred in Arroyo County that threatens to explode into riot and disorder in the streets.

ROWENA: Your Honor, of course the community is indignant. But rather than violence they have staged some peaceful demonstrations. I fail to see how that can be labeled riot and disorder.

HAROLD: Your Honor, my client has been receiving threatening phone calls.

JUDGE: I will order a change of venue in this case. Unfortunately, there are very strong racial overtones in this matter.

ROWENA: Your Honor, I submit that the question deals not so much with race as it does with justice.

JUDGE: Trial will be held in Jim Bowie County.

HAROLD: Thank you, your Honor.

BERTA: Rowena, ¿qué pasó?

ROWENA: The trial is going to be held in a mostly white, Anglo-Saxon Protestant county.

JUDGE: *(A court in Jim Bowie County.)* Now then, how many prospective jurors were called?

BAILIFF: Seventy-six, your Honor.

JUDGE: Are you satisfied with the jurors selected for this trial?

HAROLD: I certainly am, your Honor.

ROWENA: You see, Berta, the lawyers on both sides have the right to exclude, reject, any juror they want. Out of the seventy-six jurors that were called, only three were Chicanos. So the defense rejected them.

BERTA: Is that why the jury is made up of eleven Anglos and one black? It's not fair!

ROWENA: That's the way the law works. If only we would have had more registered voters who were Chicanos in this county! La

Raza doesn't vote, Berta. But don't worry, we have all the evidence we need to convict Hall. We have witnesses that heard Hall threaten to kill Danny; we also have witnesses that saw Hall try to cover up the crime. We can't lose.

BERTA: Juana, I've already lost!

ROWENA: (*To the jury.*) Cortezville, where the killing took place, is a small town in Central Texas whose population is two thousand, half of which are Mexican American. Fred Hall, the police chief, was a retired Air Force Master Sergeant who lived with his wife and daughter in a trailer home. Danny Rosales, the victim, lived with his common-law wife in a little one-room shack. He was twenty-five years old at the time of his death. Ladies and gentlemen of the jury, we intend to prove, beyond the shadow of a doubt, that Fred Hall killed Danny Rosales in cold blood and that he is guilty of first-degree murder. For my first witness, I would like to call Berta Rosales to the stand. (*Enter Berta.*) State your name, please.

BERTA: Berta López Rosales.

ROWENA: Where do you live?

BERTA: Cortezville.

ROWENA: How long have you lived there?

BERTA: Twenty-four years.

ROWENA: How did you first meet Danny Rosales?

BERTA: In a dance in a place called Chevana. It's on Highway 81.

ROWENA: What was your relationship to the deceased?

BERTA: We were living together as man and wife.

ROWENA: Were you married?

BERTA: No, when I first met him in 1967 I was too young to get married, so we just started living together. It has been seven years now.

ROWENA: When was the last time you saw your husband alive?

BERTA: On September 14, 1975, that Sunday night at our home in Cortezville.

ROWENA: Will you please tell the jury what happened there that night?

BERTA: We were watching television and getting ready to go to bed when the Deputy Sheriff drove his car up to our driveway and knocked on the front door. (*Flashback. Enter Deputy.*)

DEPUTY: Is Danny Rosales here?

BERTA: (*From the witness stand.*) "Just a minute," I said, "I'll call him. Danny! Es la policía!"

ROWENA: And what did Danny do? *(Enter Danny, dressing.)*

BERTA: He put his pants on and walked to the door.

DEPUTY: That's a mighty nice stereo and TV you got there, pardner. I'm afraid I'm going to have to take you in.

ROWENA: Do you remember what time of night this was?

BERTA: 10:45 p.m.

ROWENA: What happened then?

BERTA: He handcuffed Danny and took him to the squad car. *(To the Deputy.)* How much is the bail going to be?

DEPUTY: I don't know, fifty, one-hundred dollars.

BERTA: Please, Deputy, I don't have a car. Can you give me a ride over to my mother-in-law's so I can borrow the money?

DANNY: Berta, ellos no tienen dinero.

BERTA: Deputy, please, can't you give him another break? Can't it wait until morning?

DANNY: Berta, ¡cállate! ¡Deja de rogar! *(The Deputy leads Danny away to the squad car.)*

ROWENA: What happened then?

BERTA: The Deputy put Danny in the squad car and asked me if he could come into the house.

DEPUTY: I have some search warrants.

BERTA: He never showed them to me. And he went in the house and looked in the cabinets, in my kitchen, and stove, and in the bed . . . under the bed. Meanwhile, I was getting some clothes for Danny.

ROWENA: Can you tell us how Danny was dressed?

BERTA: Gray T-shirt, brown pants, brown shoes, black socks.

ROWENA: Did he have the shoes on when he left the house?

BERTA: No, he asked me to get them as he sat handcuffed in the squad car. That and some cigarettes. I had to light it for him. And I also put his shoes on but I didn't have time to tie them.

ROWENA: Mrs. Rosales, I will hand you what has been identified as "State's Exhibit Number 1." Would you look at that please?

BERTA: This is my husband's shoe that I put on him that night.

ROWENA: And when was the last time you saw that shoe?

BERTA: When I found it the next morning next to a pool of blood on the Old Alamo School Road.

ROWENA: Now then, getting back to this stereo and TV, how long had they been in your house?

BERTA: They had been there barely one day, since early Sunday morning.

ROWENA: And how did Danny bring them to the house?

BERTA: He and Kiki brought them in Kiki's car.

ROWENA: Who is Kiki?

BERTA: Kiki, Kiki Ventura. He used to be a friend of Danny's. They came into the house just before dawn. *(As Danny and Kiki enter.)* Danny! Where have you been? It's almost morning. I've been worried to death about you.

DANNY: Wouldn't you know it, Kiki's car broke down. We spent all night fixing it.

BERTA: Your hands are dirty. ¿Quieres algo de comer? Go wash up. I'll make some chorizo con huevos. Is that Kiki out there? Every time I see him, he's got a different car.

DANNY: Yeah, that's Kiki all right. The Chicano Robin Hood. Entrale, Kiki, Berta's not going to bite your head off.

KIKI: That's what the black widow spider said to her viejo.

BERTA: And why is Kiki the Chicano Robin Hood?

KIKI: Because I take from the rich Gringos and give to the poor Chicanos like me. Hey man, come on, I'm tired. Where do you wanna put the you-know-what?

DANNY: Shhhh!

BERTA: What are you two whispering about?

KIKI: The new stereo and TV. It's a surprise.

DANNY: It was.

BERTA: New stereo and TV!

DANNY: I rented them from a store in Dallas.

BERTA: Are you sure Señor Hood here didn't rip them off? Where did you get the money?

DANNY: Don't worry, viejita, I didn't use any of the money for la renta or la comida. This is extra feria I made picking watermelons.

KIKI: Hey, at least he didn't get it picking pockets, hey Berta?

DANNY: Kiki, go get the stuff, will you!

KIKI: Okay. Hey, Berta. ¡No te agüites! *(Exiting.)*

BERTA: Danny, I could have paid off the doctor's bill with that money. Give me the receipt, I'll ride back to Dallas con la comadre and take it back.

DANNY: Everybody else has a TV, Berta, why can't we? Ah, I haven't got it. I must have left it at the store.

BERTA: Danny, you've got to start saving your receipts, how else are we going to know how much money we spent!

DANNY: Berta!

BERTA: Danny, we'll never get out of the mess we're in unless we save and sacrifice! Si cada día nos endeudamos más y más—those debts will drag us under.

DANNY: I know you're right, it's just that everything was going so good and then . . . I got laid off. You know, all my life, we never had a TV. I used to watch color TV with this little gabachito friend. His mother would make me a roast beef sandwich. She used to say, "You probably don't get to eat roast beef at your house, do you?"

BERTA: All right, mi amor, keep the TV for a month, but what do we need a stereo for?

DANNY: That's the surprise. I know how much you like your música ranchera. I couldn't get something for me without getting something for you también.

BERTA: Danny, you could talk me into anything!

KIKI: (Entering.) Hey man, why don't you talk that stereo and TV into walking in here! Come on, that stuff is heavy . . .

ROWENA: Mrs. Rosales, I want you to tell the jury, was Danny telling the truth about having rented the stereo and TV from a firm in Dallas?

BERTA: Yes, he was. My husband didn't steal anything. He died for nothing. He was murdered!

HAROLD: Your Honor, I object. The witness is assuming that a murder has been committed.

JUDGE: Mrs. Rosales, please confine your comments to the questions at hand.

ROWENA: I would like to offer this receipt as evidence to be labeled "State's Exhibit 2."

HAROLD: I ask that the Court verify that receipt for its authenticity.

ROWENA: No further questions. Your witness, Mr. Pearl.

HAROLD: Tell us, your husband, or boyfriend, or the man you were living with, did he have a job?

BERTA: Danny had just gotten laid off from construction work.

HAROLD: What kind of education did he have?

BERTA: He went as far as the sixth grade. He quit school to go to work in the fields. His family was very poor.

HAROLD: According to his school records, Danny Rosales was a truant who was constantly in trouble, was he not?

ROWENA: I object, irrelevant and immaterial.

HAROLD: I will show the relevancy, your Honor.

JUDGE: Overruled. Answer the questions, Mrs. Rosales.

BERTA: My husband was in trouble because nobody understood him. He spoke only Spanish until he was ten. So they put him in a school for backwards children.

HAROLD: Even in his later years, wasn't your husband in constant trouble with the law?

BERTA: Only because the Sheriff was always hassling and picking on him.

HAROLD: Take a look at this photograph. Is this a fair and accurate representation of what he looked like, Danny Rosales?

BERTA: Yes, it is. But I don't know when these pictures were taken.

HAROLD: You don't? You weren't with him? What does it say here?

BERTA: "Arroyo County . . ."

HAROLD: "Arroyo County Sheriff's Department." He was charged with burglary.

ROWENA: Your Honor, again, I object, irrelevant and immaterial.

HAROLD: I will show the relevancy.

JUDGE: Overruled. But please get to the point, Mr. Pearl.

HAROLD: Now then, Mrs. Rosales, isn't it a fact that your *husband* was sentenced to three years' probation for burglary?

BERTA: I told you that Danny . . .

HAROLD: I would like a simple yes or no in response to my questions. Was he sentenced to three years' probation for burglary?

BERTA: Yes, he was.

HAROLD: Wasn't he picked up for questioning about other robberies?

BERTA: Yes.

ROWENA: Your Honor, I object, Danny Rosales is not on trial here, Fred Hall is!

HAROLD: I am establishing that Mr. Rosales had a criminal record and therefore my client had every right to question him.

JUDGE: Overruled.

ROWENA: Note my objection to the ruling.

HAROLD: Now then, Mrs. Rosales, isn't it true that your husband sold but did not deliver a calf just one month before his death?

BERTA: Yes! But he didn't steal the calf. And he didn't steal the stereo and TV. And even if he had, that was no reason to kill him!

HAROLD: Mrs. Rosales, let's go back to the night your husband was arrested. You said that the Deputy came and handcuffed your husband and put him in the squad car. What happened then?

BERTA: The Police Chief pulled up in his private car and they took him away.

HAROLD: Did you see anyone beat or push or mistreat your husband?

BERTA: No, I was in the house. It was too far away and it was dark.

HAROLD: No further questions.

BERTA: But they didn't take him to the jailhouse like they said they were . . . they took him in the opposite direction.

HAROLD: I have no further questions. You may be excused. *(Berta exits.)*

ROWENA: I would now like to call Steve Peters to the stand.

BAILIFF: Raise your right hand. Do you swear to tell the truth, the whole truth, and nothing but the truth, so help you God?

STEVE: I do.

ROWENA: State your name, please.

STEVE: Steve Earl Peters.

ROWENA: What is your relationship to Mr. Hall?

STEVE: His daughter and I are engaged to be married.

ROWENA: Why would your future father-in-law involve you in the shooting of Danny Rosales?

STEVE: I was just keeping him company.

ROWENA: You were what?

STEVE: A lot of people ride around with their police friends in town. There ain't nothing else to do.

ROWENA: What were you doing on the night of September 14, 1975?

STEVE: I was at Mr. Hall's home drinking . . . iced tea . . . and watching television.

ROWENA: And what was the reason for your being there at that time?

STEVE: I was going to ask for his daughter's hand in marriage. But I didn't get a chance to, you see. He kept getting all these calls on his police radio. Boy, he was on duty twenty-four hours per day. For instance, the night before, I was with him on a stakeout hoping to catch this Danny Rosales transporting some stolen goods . . . *(Flashback.)*

FRED: Keep your eyes peeled for a '69 burgundy Mustang, Stevie, I don't want 'er slipping by us.

STEVE: Don'tcha worry, Chief, I got eyes like an eagle.

FRED: Where in the heck could they be? That stool pigeon said they'd be here three hours ago.

STEVE: Yeah, we sure been waiting here a long time. These skeeters are something else. Say, Chief, as long as we're waiting out here, doing nothing, how's about if I ask you a real personal question.

FRED: Wait a minute! What if they took the back road into town?

STEVE: Nah, this is the only direct road from Dallas. Now, I was thinking, I just got promoted to Assistant Manager of the Tasty Freeze. I got my pickup truck all paid off and I just saw this out-of-sight apartment near the Cielito Lindo mall . . .

FRED: Wait, that informer said tonight. But did he mean late night, early evening or even late afternoon? You know how they talk in Spanish—they say evening when they mean afternoon!

STEVE: Gee, Mr. Hall, you must want this guy awful bad to stay out here all night waiting for him.

FRED: I'll tell you, Stevie, this is the last time that two-bit thief is going to pull the wool over my eyes. Every time a house gets broken into, he's seen in the vicinity. But every time I go and pick him up for questioning, he's managed to dispose of the goods. Or else he's got a phony alibi. I'm sick and tired of chasing him.

STEVE: Are you sure this here informer is telling the truth?

FRED: He's been right on three different occasions. And we prosecuted all three times. You see, the man is a thief himself. But I got him under control. I even pay him out of my own back pocket.

STEVE: Well, sounds like you oughta teach that Rosales a lesson, Chief.

FRED: I will. I'll teach him a lesson he'll never forget.

STEVE: Say, Chief, if you don't mind my asking, how come you want me coming along with you on these stakeouts?

FRED: Well, Stevie, if you're going to be my son-in-law . . .

STEVE: Wow, Chief, do you really mean it?

FRED: But forget about that Tasty Freeze, Stevie, that's kid stuff. You need a job with a future, one that'll make a man out of you. (*Handing Steve the shotgun.*)

STEVE: Oh, wow, you don't mean . . .

FRED: Why not law enforcement? I could use a new deputy. The one I have now ain't worth a damn.

STEVE: (*Pointing the shotgun at the audience.*) Will you show me how to use this? (*Fade out.*)

GRACE: (*At the home of Fred Hall.*) Debbie! Did you get those spots scrubbed away?

DEBBIE: Mother, I scoured until my fingers ached.

GRACE: You just have to scrub harder, dear.

DEBBIE: But I'm scraping the finish off the pan, which is why the food sticks to it.

GRACE: Nonsense, you polish it until it shines like a mirror. Then, someday, God willing, when you and Stevie have your own home, your kitchen will be as spic and span as mine. Your dishes will be washed after each meal, the table wiped off, the sink shiny white.

DEBBIE: Oh Mom, that's disgusting!

GRACE: What is, dear?

DEBBIE: That whole domestic scene. I mean, the Lord didn't create me to spend the rest of my life in a kitchen cooking for Mr. Stevie Peters, that's for sure.

GRACE: Debbie, darling, a woman's role is with her man. Why do you think Eve was made from the rib of Adam? Besides, aren't you kinda sweet on Stevie?

DEBBIE: Oh gee, it was strictly a high school romance. He was the quarterback of the football team. He's all right, I guess. But I don't want to spend the rest of my life with the manager of the Tasty Freeze.

GRACE: Don't worry, once he comes into this family, your Daddy'll set him straight.

DEBBIE: Mama, you don't understand. I want to go to school and have a career. I don't want to be a dumb old housewife all my life. Oh, don't get me wrong. I'm not putting you down. You just don't realize your own worth. Cooking and cleaning and raising kids is a full-time job and you don't even get paid for it.

GRACE: Debbie, of course I get paid. Not with a check, but with love. And who do you think bought this trailer home and everything in it? Including your little subcompact, young lady.

DEBBIE: Daddy did, of course. And I'm very grateful. I've seen the way some of these black and Mexican kids live and it just about breaks my heart. I guess what I'm trying to say is, I won't have time to be cooking and cleaning and taking care of kids because I'll be too busy working for me.

GRACE: Debbie, listen to me, I know for a fact that this very night Stevie is going to ask your father for your hand in marriage.

DEBBIE: Do you know what? I think weddings are silly. They're like the opposite of a funeral.

GRACE: Debbie, you're just nervous. But wait until you walk down that aisle, with the organ music and the assembled guests, in the eyes of God.

DEBBIE: God!

GRACE: Don't you use the Lord's name in vain! Honey, your Daddy and Stevie are home.

DEBBIE: (*Out of hearing range.*) Jesus Christ!

STEVE: Hi, Mrs. Hall!

GRACE: Hello, Stevie dear.

STEVE: Debbie, can I talk to you for a minute?

DEBBIE: (*Going to her father.*) How's my Lone Ranger?

FRED: Not too good, honey, Tonto and me let the wild injuns get away.

STEVE: Debbie.

DEBBIE: Did you play Tonto tonight, Stevie? Hey, do you know that "Tonto" means dumb in Spanish?

FRED: That's pretty funny, eh kimo sabe?

STEVE: Yeah. Hey Debbie, I gotta tell you something.

DEBBIE: What?

STEVE: Your Daddy said we could get married.

DEBBIE: Wonderful.

GRACE: What's the matter Fred, are you all right?

FRED: I'm okay. Hand me my painkillers. I've been trying to catch this little weasel for days.

GRACE: Fred, forget it, stay home, this is your weekend off.

FRED: No, no, no. I got a hot tip from an informant. I got this character right between the crossbars. Any news from the police radio?

GRACE: Oh, can't we turn this off, even for one night? You're not going out again, you've been getting home so late. And that big bed gets awful cold with only one body warming it.

FRED: My painkillers. Get me my painkillers.

DEBBIE: I'll get 'em for you, Daddy.

GRACE: Debbie, there's a nice tall pitcher of iced tea in the refrigerator. Fix everybody a cold glass.

STEVE: What's the matter with the Chief?

GRACE: He ain't been the same ever since that shoot-out with the two blacks in the liquor store. Did you know that he was wounded three times?

STEVE: I never heard the whole story.

GRACE: Fred was on patrol when he noticed this suspicious looking car parked out in front of Del's Liquor Store. As he went up to the front door two colored guys ran out.

FRED: One went left and one went right. The one on the left I caught and handcuffed. Just then I noticed a colored lady in the car. I ordered her out and was trying to get help through the dispatcher when the other colored guy came up behind me and stuck a knife to my throat.

GRACE: The first colored fellow that Fred had apprehended started hitting him on the head with a rock and with the handcuffs.

FRED: I kind of went semi-conscious and hit the ground as one of them started shooting at me. I rolled over and over on the floor to avoid being shot.

GRACE: They shot him three times.

FRED: Here, I'll show you.

GRACE: No, Fred, please, don't take off your shirt again!

DEBBIE: Oh, Daddy!

GRACE: (At the witness stand.) And that is why my husband has to take painkillers to this day.

HAROLD: What kind of painkillers does Fred take?

GRACE: Valium and percodan.

HAROLD: Have you noticed anything unusual about your husband since this unfortunate accident occurred?

GRACE: I've noticed that his memory has gotten bad. He has also been depressed, moody and given to fits of bad temper.

HAROLD: How long have you been married to the defendant?

GRACE: For twenty-two years.

HAROLD: Anything else about your husband involving his line of work?

GRACE: He tended to do things that were risky, extra risky. If he thought he was going into some dangerous place to apprehend a criminal or if there might be other people there, he would go in and do it. Or if there was a traffic offender on the highway, he would address them while they sat in their car, a practice which is considered dangerous. He said he felt that he didn't care whether any of these people might shoot him or not. And one day he told me he looked forward to being killed in the line of duty.

HAROLD: Anything else, Mrs. Hall? I know that this is painful, but we've got to get this out so everybody will know what kind of condition your husband was in.

GRACE: Well, he became very cold towards me in our personal relationship. It's not that he didn't love me, I could feel that, it's just that he stopped becoming intimate with me. After Fred almost died in that shootout, he said he wanted to rededicate himself to his career in law. He saw himself as someone saving the community from violence, bringing Christ to couples who got into marital conflicts, and ridding the community of drug addicts and thieves so that his children and grandchildren could grow up in a decent community.

ROWENA: Your Honor, I am going to object to this. Didn't we go over this material during the Sanity Hearing?

JUDGE: Sustained.

HAROLD: Thank you, Mrs. Hall, thank you for telling us what kind of a husband and father Fred Hall is. Your witness, Ms. Saldivar.

ROWENA: I have no questions at this time.

JUDGE: You may step down, Mrs. Hall.

BERTA: Aren't you going to question her? She made him out to be a saint.

ROWENA: This is not the time, Berta. We'll get to her and her daughter later.

BERTA: Why didn't they charge her with murder? She helped him to bury Danny's body!

ROWENA: Siéntate, Berta, please, you're making it worse for our case.

HAROLD: I would now like to call Kiki Ventura to the stand. *(Enter Kiki.)*

BAILIFF: Do you swear to tell the truth, the whole truth, and nothing but the truth, so help you God?

KIKI: Yeah, I guess so.

JUDGE: You mean, "yes," don't you, Mr. Ventura?

KIKI: Yes, sir.

HAROLD: Please state your name, age and occupation.

KIKI: Enrique Ventura. But everybody calls me Kiki. I'm almost thirty years old and, uh, what else did you ask me?

HAROLD: Your occupation.

KIKI: Yeah, well, right now, I'm unemployed.

HAROLD: Mr. Ventura, what was your relationship to the deceased, Danny Rosales?

KIKI: He was my friend.

HAROLD: You were also a business associate of Mr. Rosales, were you not? Didn't you move different items of furniture and things like that from one county to another?

KIKI: Nah, nothing like that.

HAROLD: Mr. Ventura, is it not a proven fact that you have quite an extensive criminal record?

KIKI: Yes, but that was in the past, I don't do that anymore. Ask my parole officer.

HAROLD: You and Danny were just good drinking buddies, huh?

KIKI: Yeah, we would pop a few cold cans of what they call Colorado kool ade.

HAROLD: Now then, Mr. Ventura, were you ever involved in the sale of narcotics?

KIKI: I refuse to answer that on the grounds that it might incriminal me.

HAROLD: Mr. Ventura, just answer my question, yes or no.

KIKI: Don't I have the right to talk to my lawyers?

JUDGE: Answer the questions, Mr. Ventura.

KIKI: Yes, but I served my time.

HAROLD: Now then, isn't it also a fact that you and Mr. Rosales sold a calf and then did not deliver it?

KIKI: No, no, that's not true! Danny sold that calf, not me. No, you can't pin that on me. It was Danny. *(Flashback.)*

DANNY: Kiki, when am I going to get the feria? The farmer wants his money back.

KIKI: Shit, Danny, I'm kind of broke right now. All I got is half a kilo of grass. Acapulco Gold. Worth about $200. You want it?

DANNY: No, I don't.

KIKI: You could sell it to some Gringo college student for $300 easy.

DANNY: I'm not dealing any dope.

KIKI: Well then, let's smoke it!

DANNY: I'm through getting wasted.

KIKI: Hey man, are you turning into a Boy Scout?

DANNY: No, but I'm going to start using my head to think, instead of using it to beat my brains against the wall.

KIKI: What are you going to do, man, go to college or something?

DANNY: Yeah, what's wrong with that? I'm going to get my G.E.D. and then go to the junior college.

KIKI: Come on, man, you been talking to your old lady again? She's been telling you how you could have been a brain surgeon!

DANNY: No, Kiki, I've been talking to myself. And I've decided that twenty-six years old is too old to be playing in the streets, man. I don't want to give Berta a bunch of kids just to watch them do a rerun of my own life. No ves, I'm sick of being poor and of the alcohol and of the food stamps.

KIKI: Hey, well excuse me! What are you gonna do, go live with the Gringos in their part of town?

DANNY: No, but I'm not going to live like a punk kid, either.

KIKI: Simón vato, you do your own thing. (*Turning to go.*) Later.

DANNY: Hey, Kiki, we're still friends, que no?

KIKI: Sure . . .

DEPUTY: (*Entering.*) Which one of you is Danny Rosales?

KIKI: He is.

DEPUTY: I'm Deputy Davis. I have a warrant for your arrest on the charge that you sold but did not deliver a calf. A farmer named Kramer signed the complaint.

KIKI: Hay te watcho, Danny . . .

DANNY: Wait a minute, Kiki, you got some explaining to do.

DEPUTY: No, I think you better start explaining, Rosales.

DANNY: Well, you see, Deputy, I couldn't deliver the calf because Kiki here took it and killed it.

KIKI: Yeah, I killed it, but it was an accident, an emergency.

DEPUTY: An accident?

KIKI: Well, you see, I was trying to fatten it up for him. It was a little underweight, so my Abuelita says to me, "Kiki, that calf looks a little sickly, maybe you should feed it some of this special grain." So I did. A week passes, three weeks passes. One day I wake up and, boom, the calf is patas para arriba, dead. I was feeding it locoweed by mistake. You don't believe me?

DANNY: Tell him what you did with it, Kiki.

KIKI: I ate it.

DEPUTY: Look, whatever the reason, Rosales, you are still responsible. So, when are you going to give Farmer Kramer his money back?

DANNY: I already gave half of it back last week. And I'm going to give him another fifty tonight. I promise to pay back every penny.

DEPUTY: Why should I believe you?

DANNY: Because I don't want to go to jail. Also, if I'm in jail I can't work. And if I can't work, I'll never pay him back.

DEPUTY: That's a good point. I'll tell you what, if you promise to pay $50 a week until you pay off the entire amount, I won't take you in.

DANNY: Thanks a lot, Deputy.

KIKI: Hey man, I wish all the chotas could be like you!

DEPUTY: I don't want to lock you up, Rosales, but if you miss just one payment . . .

DANNY: Don't worry, I won't. Thanks for the break, Deputy!

KIKI: Orale pues! Lemme show you the Chicano handshake. (*Going to the Deputy.*)

DEPUTY: (*Ignoring Kiki.*) Don't let me down, Rosales. (*Goes to witness stand.*)

KIKI: Pinche pig!

DANNY: Ya ves, Kiki. My luck is changing already! Pero now you know how much I really need that money.

KIKI: Don't worry, you'll get it, you'll get every bit of it. (*Exits.*)

ROWENA: Deputy Davis, can you tell us what happened that Sunday night when you went to arrest Danny Rosales at his home?

DEPUTY: Chief Hall had left instructions for me to serve that theft warrant charge against Rosales.

ROWENA: And when you arrest someone you routinely call into the dispatcher, do you not?

DEPUTY: Yes, Ma'am.

ROWENA: That must have been how Fred Hall knew you were arresting Danny Rosales at exactly 10:30 P.M.

DEPUTY: Yes, that is the only way he could have known.

ROWENA: In other words, Chief Hall used the misdemeanor theft warrant as an excuse to take Danny out to the Old Alamo School Road to beat him up and shoot him.

HAROLD: Your Honor, I object to this line of questioning.

JUDGE: Sustained! Miss Saldivar, this court is interested in facts, not assumptions. (*Flashback.*)

DEPUTY: That's a might nice stereo and TV you got there, pardner. Maybe you should have used that money to finish paying off that farmer.

DANNY: But I only missed one payment.

DEPUTY: Danny, you have the right to remain silent. You have the right to an attorney. Anything you say may be used against you.

ROWENA: What happened after you read the suspect his rights and searched the house?

DEPUTY: I was getting ready to take him in when Fred Hall pulled up in his private car.

DEPUTY: Okay, Danny, let's go.

FRED: (*Entering.*) Was the stolen stereo and TV in the house, Davis?

DANNY: Stolen?

DEPUTY: Yes, it was. Who is that with you, Fred?

FRED: None of your damn business. All right, Rosales, where did an unemployed Mexican like you who lives in a broken-down shack like this, which ain't even got a telephone, get a brand new stereo and TV?

DANNY: I rented them in Dallas.

FRED: He rented them in Dallas. Huh. Have you got a receipt?

DANNY: No, I don't, you see, I . . .

FRED: You what! You what! *(Striking Danny.)* Don't lie to me, boy!

DANNY: I'm telling the truth. I rented them from a store.

FRED: You lying piece of shit! *(Kicking Danny to the floor.)* I've had just about enough of you! Stevie, gimme that shotgun. *(Jabbing Danny with the shotgun.)* Now then, are you going to tell me the truth, are you going to confess? I'll kill you, boy!

DEPUTY: Come on, Danny, tell the truth. You don't want Chief Hall to get all upset, do you?

DANNY: I didn't do anything wrong.

FRED: Let the thieving son of a bitch go! Uncuff him and let him run so I can shoot him!

DANNY: I swear to you! I rented them from a store in Dallas.

FRED: I'm gonna kill you! I'm gonna kill you! *(Beating him.)*

DEPUTY: Hey, Fred, what the hell's got into you?

FRED: You lying to me, boy. You've been lying to me all along! But I got you this time . . . dead to rights.

DEPUTY: Take it easy, Fred.

FRED: Davis, put him in the squad car. Let's go to the Old Alamo School Road, maybe his tongue will loosen up along the way.

DEPUTY: Couldn't we just lock him up overnight and call the rental place in the morning?

FRED: Davis, how long you been a law enforcement officer in Arroyo County?

DEPUTY: Six months.

FRED: And you're the dumb son of a bitch who let him go in the first place. What are you, a social worker! I've been doing this for six years.

DEPUTY: But Fred, you can't be beating a prisoner like that.

FRED: I'm only trying to scare him into confessing. Now, play along with me. Tell him I'm going to shoot him if he doesn't tell the truth. I used to do this all the time in the Civilian Investigation Division.

DEPUTY: Okay, Fred, we'll try it your way.

FRED: I'll follow you in my car. And don't let him go this time. Asshole!

ROWENA: Then, you actually heard Fred Hall threaten to kill Danny Rosales? *(Back at the witness stand.)*

DEPUTY: Yes, I did.

ROWENA: How many times?

DEPUTY: At least five times.

ROWENA: Take note: Deputy Davis heard Fred Hall threaten to kill Danny Rosales at least five times that night. No further questions at this time. I pass the witness.

HAROLD: Deputy Davis, what was your exact title out there in Cortezville? Didn't you call yourself Assistant Chief Deputy?

DEPUTY: I believe the title was Deputy Chief of Police.

HAROLD: You had aspirations of becoming Chief of Police, did you not?

DEPUTY: Well, every police officer has ambitions of bettering himself.

HAROLD: You didn't get along with Chief Hall at all, did you?

DEPUTY: We weren't exactly the best of friends. But I never let this get in the way of our work.

HAROLD: Now, that night at the Rosales' home, when you asked Fred who he was with, why did he respond, "none of your damn business?"

DEPUTY: I guess I wasn't supposed to know.

HAROLD: Yet you just told me that in no way did your personal feelings for each other get in the way of your professional duties, is that right?

DEPUTY: Yes, sir.

HAROLD: Okay. Those threats he made to Danny Rosales, things like, "I'm going to kill you," and things of that nature, he told you that was just a bluff, did he not?

DEPUTY: He tried to convince me it was just a bluff.

HAROLD: But you had no reason to doubt that, did you?

DEPUTY: At that time, I had no reason, no, sir.

HAROLD: That was just a ploy to get information out of a suspected burglar, was it not?

DEPUTY: I don't approve of it.

HAROLD: He told you that this was an accepted tactic, this ploy or bluff, in the Civilian Investigation Division of the United States Air Force, did he not?

DEPUTY: He did, but I really wouldn't know about the legality of that.

HAROLD: You wouldn't know, would you? Were you ever enrolled in a police officer's training academy or anything of that sort prior to being hired in Cortezville?

DEPUTY: No, sir, I was not. But I plan to go, sir.

HAROLD: No further questions. I would now like to call Fred Hall to the stand.

BAILIFF: Raise your right hand. Do you swear to tell the truth, the whole truth, and nothing but the truth, so help you God?

FRED: I do.

HAROLD: Tell us your name please.

FRED: Fred Harold Hall.

HAROLD: Mr. Hall, I would like for you to tell the jury a little bit about your background, specifically your involvement with any previous police work.

FRED: Well, I retired from the United States Air Force in 1969 after thirty years of service. I was a Senior Master Sergeant assigned to the Civilian Investigation Division.

HAROLD: You also served in combat in World War II, the Korean Conflict, and the Vietnam Conflict . . .

ROWENA: Immaterial and irrelevant.

JUDGE: Sustained.

HAROLD: Let's move on to another point. Back to the night of September 12, Friday. Do you recall receiving information from an informant?

FRED: Yes, sir, it was information pertaining to Danny Rosales . . .

ROWENA: Objection, hearsay.

HAROLD: I'm not going into what the informant said, Your Honor, I just wanted to know if he was reliable.

JUDGE: Proceed.

HAROLD: Now then, was the informant reliable in the past?

FRED: Yes, sir, in three different cases we got three different convictions.

HAROLD: Now then, the outstanding theft warrant, that business about the calf. Why did you decide to activate that warrant against Rosales?

FRED: I hoped to use it to stop a vehicle that was supposedly driven by Rosales and which supposedly contained stolen property.

HAROLD: But you weren't out to "get" Rosales, were you?

FRED: No, there were just all these trails leading to him.

HAROLD: And did you ever make any disparaging remarks about Mexicans or Chicanos in general?

FRED: No, I have a great deal of respect for Mexicans and I have many Mexican friends.

HAROLD: Now then, that Sunday night, September 14th, why did you take your future son-in-law with you, besides just for the company?

FRED: Well, I had been taking him along regularly, to show him what police work was like. But that particular night I asked him to come along in case I needed a witness in the event that Deputy Davis had erred. I wanted to show his error in police work because he had erred so badly in the past.

HAROLD: All right, tell us what happened when you went to arrest Danny Rosales at his home.

FRED: Well, as Stevie and I pulled into the driveway we saw the Deputy struggling to get Rosales into his squad car. *(Flashback.)*

DANNY: God damn it, let me go!

DEPUTY: I should have never given you a break, Rosales.

FRED: Have you read the suspect his rights, Deputy?

DEPUTY: Yes, sir.

FRED: Good. Now, Danny, could you please tell us where you got the new stereo and television?

DEPUTY: It's a Curtis Mathis.

DANNY: ¡Qué chingaos te importa, pinche güey!

FRED: What did he say, Deputy?

DEPUTY: I don't know, Chief, but it don't sound too good.

FRED: Danny, I hate to do this, but I'm afraid we're going to have to take you down to the station.

DEPUTY: You ain't taking me nowhere!

FRED: Put him in the squad car, Davis. Danny Rosales, are you resisting arrest?

DANNY: ¡Hijos de puta! Police brutality!

FRED: Davis, why don't we take the long way to the jailhouse. Maybe Danny will calm down by the time we get there.

DEPUTY: Good idea, Chief. *(Blackout.)*

HAROLD: And so, you took him down to the Old Alamo School Road to try and talk to him on a personal level, sort of like how a father might relate to his son.

ROWENA: Your Honor, I object, the defense is leading the witness.

JUDGE: Objection sustained.

HAROLD: Very well, then, in your own words, tell us what happened that night.

FRED: The Deputy had left. Stevie was in the car. Rosales and I were by the side of the road. I was still trying to question him.

HAROLD: Now, as a result of this questioning, did he make any gestures towards you?

FRED: Yes, sir, he started coming closer to me and making threatening gestures and I had to push him back.

HAROLD: You had to protect yourself?

FRED: Yes, sir. He tried to grab a hold of the shotgun. But I wasn't going to let him have it, not if I could help it.

HAROLD: Show us how Rosales grabbed the shotgun.

FRED: Like this. He grabbed the barrel and tried to yank it away from me. Then he kicked me. At one point I was off my feet. I'd been kicked just above the pelvis. I was down on one knee.

HAROLD: Mr. Hall, tell us, did you have fear and apprehension for your life?

FRED: I certainly did. The thought flashed back in my mind how my gun had been taken away from me before and how I had been shot three times.

HAROLD: So here was this taller, younger, stronger man kicking you and trying to take your shotgun away. Go on.

ROWENA: Your Honor, the defense is leading the witness again.

JUDGE: Overruled. Continue!

ROWENA: Note my exception to the ruling.

FRED: Thinking about that earlier fight made me struggle all the further. It was dark, he tried to yank the gun away and it went off . . .

HAROLD: Yes . . .

FRED: Accidentally.

HAROLD: Mr. Hall, I want you to look the jury right in the eye. Did you intentionally pull the trigger of that shotgun, sir?

FRED: As God is my witness, I never intended to pull the trigger and hurt that man!

HAROLD: Ladies and gentlemen, I ask you, does this man sitting here look capable of murdering in cold blood?

BERTA: He's lying! He's lying! He murdered Danny, he murdered him!

JUDGE: Mrs. Rosales, sit down or I will be forced to remove you from this court.

BERTA: He's a killer! You're going to let him get away with it!

JUDGE: Order, order in this court! Bailiff, remove Mrs. Rosales!

ROWENA: Your Honor, I see no need to have Mrs. Rosales physically removed from this court!

JUDGE: Don't you raise your voice to me, Miss Saldivar! This court will recess for ten minutes.

ROWENA: Your Honor, I have not yet cross-examined the witness!

JUDGE: Court is recessed for ten minutes!

ROWENA: Your Honor! I protest!

ACT II

JUDGE: Miss Saldivar, before continuing the proceedings, I want it made perfectly clear that you are to refrain from any further outbursts in this court, is that understood.

ROWENA: Your Honor, I apologize for having raised my voice in court.

JUDGE: You may proceed, Miss Saldivar.

ROWENA: Now then, Mr. Hall, how long did you work for the City of Cortezville as Chief of Police?

FRED: Approximately six years.

ROWENA: What was your salary at the time you were released?

FRED: $450 per month.

ROWENA: $450 per month. That's not very much for a family of three, is it?

HAROLD: This is irrelevant, your Honor.

ROWENA: I will show the relevancy.

JUDGE: Proceed.

ROWENA: You had to supplement your income with your pension from the Air Force, did you not?

FRED: Yes, I did.

ROWENA: Now, you never went to a professional police training academy prior to being hired by the City of Cortezville, did you?

FRED: No, I did not.

ROWENA: And when you worked for the Civilian Investigation Division of the Air Force, you were a clerk, were you not?

FRED: Yes, but I . . .

ROWENA: You only worked for them for two years in a clerical capacity, according to your records. Isn't it a fact that the Air Force stationed you at many different jobs in different places during your thirty-year stint?

FRED: Yes, it was.

ROWENA: Isn't it a fact that small Texas towns hire retired servicemen because they are the only ones who can afford to take the relatively low-paying jobs?

HAROLD: That is not a fact, that is an assumption.

JUDGE: Sustained. The jury will ignore that assumption.

ROWENA: Now then, Mr. Hall, in spite of the fact that you had no formal training in police work, you claim that you performed your duties as police chief according to the letter of the law, correct?

FRED: As to the best of my ability.

ROWENA: Then why did you take Danny Rosales to a deserted country road five miles outside of town to interrogate him? Why didn't you take him to your office inside the police station?

FRED: I took him out there because I had every intention of letting him go. I just did it to scare him.

ROWENA: While you were out there in that woodsy, rural area, did you notice any houses?

FRED: Yes, I did.

ROWENA: There were houses. Is that the reason you didn't want any lights turned on?

FRED: I don't recall that.

ROWENA: You don't recall that?

FRED: No.

ROWENA: You don't recall asking Steve Peters where you could bury the body before it even got cold?

FRED: No, I don't.

ROWENA: You don't recall talking to your wife about taking the body to east Texas?

FRED: No, I don't.

ROWENA: Do you mean to tell the ladies and gentlemen of this jury that you don't recall driving around town with the body in the back seat of your automobile?

FRED: No, I don't.

ROWENA: Your Honor, please instruct the witness to answer the questions!

JUDGE: Mr. Hall, I don't need to remind you that you are under oath. Do you or do you not remember what happend that night?

FRED: Your Honor, I can't recall anything that happened after the gun went off. My mind is a total blank.

HAROLD: Your Honor, if I may interject a word here. Mrs. Hall testified earlier regarding my client's loss of memory due to the trauma of the wounds which he suffered in that shoot-out.

ROWENA: I insist that the witness answer my questions in full!

HAROLD: Your Honor, competent physicians have testified that the defendant, Fred Hall, has Alzheimer's Disease or pre-senile dementia. He is a sick man, your Honor.

JUDGE: Mr. Hall, I want you to answer the questions to the best of your ability. Proceed, Miss Saldivar.

ROWENA: All right, let's talk about this so-called beating on your head, Mr. Hall. Did you have any x-rays taken?

FRED: No, I did not.

ROWENA: You mean to say that the doctors didn't think it was important to take x-rays of your head and yet you claim that this is the cause of your amnesia five years later?

FRED: The bullet wounds to my body were the more serious. The problems with my head turned up later.

ROWENA: Now, you testified, and I quote, "as God is my witness, I did not intend to kill that man." How come your thoughts are so clear on that point, yet on other points, points that are damaging to your case, you can't recall.

FRED: Well, as I indicated, my thoughts, even right now, are real scrambled because of the medication I am obliged to take. But I truly believe that it was an accident.

ROWENA: You believe it was an accident. Are you saying you don't know for sure?

FRED: I am saying that the whole thing has gone all kinds of ways through my mind. I even dream about it. I can't actually say yes or no and be positive one way or another, but this is what I feel in my heart.

ROWENA: You only recall the things that you think will help you, but you don't recall the things you think will hurt, right?

FRED: No, that is not correct.

ROWENA: That's what it sounds like to me, Mr. Hall!

HAROLD: I will object to her arguing with the witness, Your Honor.

JUDGE: Disregard the statement, "it sounds like it."

ROWENA: Very well, Mr. Hall, you may step down. Let me call some witnesses who will help you refresh your memory. I would like to recall Steve Earl Peters to the stand. *(Enter Steve.)* Steve, do you know what an indictment is?

STEVE: That is when someone is charged with a crime.

ROWENA: Are you charged with a crime now by indictment?

STEVE: Yes, I am.

ROWENA: Do you also understand that you are still under oath and that perjury is a punishable offense?

HAROLD: Your Honor, I object, the Prosecution is intimidating the witness.

JUDGE: Objection sustained. Watch your line of questioning, counsel.

ROWENA: Steve, let's go back to that weekend at the home of Fred Hall, prior to Danny Rosales' arrest. *(Flashback.)*

STEVE: Well, we got back from the stakeout late Saturday night. We all sat down and had a cold drink. Of course, I was so excited I could hardly wait to tell Debbie about the wedding.

DEBBIE: Hi, Daddy!

STEVE: Hey, honey pie, guess what! I talked to your Dad!

DEBBIE: Oh, Stevie, you didn't!

STEVE: He said we could get married!

DEBBIE: Wonderful!

FRED: This calls for a drink.

GRACE: Have you set a date for the wedding?

ROWENA: *(From the side.)* How many drinks did you have, Steve?

STEVE: Oh, about three or four. Debbie, I'm going to make you the happiest woman alive!

ROWENA: Exactly what were you drinking?

STEVE: Margaritas! Margaritas! We drank until dawn. How many kids do you want to have?

DEBBIE: Oh, Stevie, lots and lots!

ROWENA: What did you do when you got up?

STEVE: We had some lunch. Then we started drinking again.

ROWENA: Was Fred drinking margaritas that day?

STEVE: No, not margaritas, iced tea! He was drinking iced tea.

ROWENA: You're under oath, Steve.

STEVE: Yes, he was drinking margaritas.

ROWENA: All night and all day and then that night again?

STEVE: Yes.

ROWENA: What kind of condition was he in?

STEVE: He wasn't drunk or anything, he could really hold his liquor.

ROWENA: Was Fred Hall consuming anything other than margaritas that weekend?

GRACE: Fred, what are you doing? You know the doctor told you not to drink and take painkillers at the same time. *(Fadeout.)*

ROWENA: In other words, ladies and gentlemen of the jury, Fred Hall was taking painkillers and washing them down with margaritas for two days prior to Danny Rosales' arrest. And now, Steve, tell us what happened when you pulled into Rosales' driveway that night.

STEVE: The Chief got out of the car and arrested Danny.

ROWENA: Did he beat him?

STEVE: Yeah, I guess so.

ROWENA: Brutally?

HAROLD: Objection.

JUDGE: Sustained.

ROWENA: Did you participate in that beating?

STEVE: Heck no, I was just holding the shotgun.

ROWENA: Did you point the shotgun at Danny Rosales?

STEVE: No! In fact, the Chief took the gun away from me and pointed it at Danny's head.

ROWENA: Is that when Hall threatened to kill Rosales?

STEVE: Yes. We were out by the Old Alamo School Road waiting for Davis to bring the prisoner. *(Flashback.)* Hey, Chief, how come you hit that Meskin so hard?

FRED: You see, Stevie, when you're dealing with these people you gotta be real firm. This *(Holding shotgun.)* is the only language they understand. You gotta get 'em to respect you. And to do that you gotta put the fear a God in 'em.

STEVE: He looked *real* scared. I'll bet he'll come around to talking any minute.

FRED: I'll tell you something, these damn people breed like rabbits and end up having fifteen kids and living on welfare. I don't know how they do it. Before long they'll outnumber us. What we oughta do is deport them. Don't make no difference if they was born here or not. Now this particular guy here is the worst of the lot. Did I tell you that I seen him eyeing Debbie?

STEVE: Eyeing her? What do you mean, eyeing her?

FRED: He was following her around. One time, after I dropped her off at the bus station, I got back in the car and as the bus was pulling away I saw her waving to me. Rosales was sitting next to her, grinning at me.

STEVE: That damn chile dipper!

FRED: *(To the Deputy as he brings Danny in.)* Well, it's about time you got here! We've been waiting half the night. Now, for the last time, where did you get that stereo and TV?

DANNY: Mr. Hall, you are making a big mistake. I rented them from a store in Dallas.

FRED: You lying son of a bitch! *(Striking Danny.)* Unhandcuff him. Davis, let him run so I can shoot him!

DEPUTY: Hey, come on, Fred that's enough!

FRED: I said unhandcuff him! That's an order!

DEPUTY: All right, let me have the flashlight here so I can see what I am doing.

FRED: No, no flashlight. I don't want no lights.

DEPUTY: *(Down on his knees trying to unhandcuff Danny.)* But I can't see to get the handcuffs off him.

FRED: Steve, close that door! I don't want no car lights, no flashlights, no cigarettes. I killed me a Meskin before and I am fixing to kill me another one.

DEPUTY: There, I got the handcuffs off of him. Now what are you going to do?

FRED: Go back to Cortezville, Davis.

DEPUTY: Fred, stop this shit, it ain't working!

FRED: I'm taking over now!

DEPUTY: But he's my prisoner!

FRED: *(Threatening the Deputy with the shotgun.)* Fuck you! Now, git! *(Deputy exits the murder scene and walks into another space, pacing.)* Now then, Mr. Rosales . . . *(Leading Danny aside.)*

ROWENA: *(Her voice.)* What was going through your mind when the police chief threatened you with the shotgun and told you to go back to Cortezville?

DEPUTY: *(As though he were testifying or thinking out loud.)* Being relatively new on the job and all, I was thinking that maybe he was trying to put me through some kind of test or play some kind of game to see how sharp I was. He had mentioned several times before that he was going to test me to see if I was good enough to stay in the department.

ROWENA: So you disobeyed his order? *(Her voice.)*

DEPUTY: Yes. I had the feeling, an intuition, that something was wrong. I drove about 200 yards or so down the road, cut the radio and lights off, and sat there about two or three minutes. That's when I heard what sounded like a shot. *(Shot is heard.)*

ROWENA: *(Voice.)* Now, Steve, you were in the car. Could you see what was happening out there?

STEVE: Pretty well. The moon was pretty bright that night. They were standing behind the car, two or three feet away from each other, talking back and forth. Mr. Hall pushed him with the butt of the gun and then with the barrel of the gun.

ROWENA: What did Danny Rosales do?

STEVE: He pushed the barrel of the gun away. Mr. Hall went towards him and then I heard the shot.

ROWENA: *(Voice.)* Did you see what happened?

STEVE: No, they were in my blind spot. *(To Fred.)* What was that? Fred! Fred!

FRED: He wrestled with the gun, Stevie. It went off . . . and it killed him.

STEVE: Jesus, what are you going to do now?

FRED: I don't know, it was an accident, but nobody will ever believe me.

STEVE: Let's get the hell outa here!

FRED: Wait. There's a light! Somebody's coming. Move away from here. (*They walk in the direction of the Deputy.*)

DEPUTY: What happened? I heard a shot. Fred, where's Rosales? I want to know right now, the bullshit's over.

FRED: Stevie, uh, get back in the car. Come here, Davis, I want to tell you something.

DEPUTY: Just cut the bullshit, Fred. What's going on? Where's Rosales?

FRED: If you just shut up, I'll tell you. Well, Davis, I, uh, killed him!

DEPUTY: You what? How did you do it? What happened, where is he?

FRED: No, I didn't kill him. I was just blowing smoke at you. I just winged him is all.

DEPUTY: Where did you "wing" him?

FRED: Right up here, under the left armpit. But hey, he's all right.

DEPUTY: What the hell are you talking about?

FRED: I was just joking.

DEPUTY: I said cut the bullshit. What did you do to Rosales?

FRED: I'll tell you the truth. He tripped me and I fell. That's when the gun went off accidentally. Then he ran away.

DEPUTY: Which way did he go?

FRED: He ran into the woods. He's all right. I just scared him.

DEPUTY: God damn it! You better tell me the truth, Fred.

FRED: I am. Look for yourself. This is the spot where he took off from. If he's here, he'd be in that ditch.

DEPUTY: Come on down here, help me look. (*Fred makes no effort to look.*)

FRED: Is he there?

DEPUTY: I don't see anything.

FRED: He's probably on his way home right now.

DEPUTY: Are you telling me the truth? Why did you tell me you killed him?

FRED: I was just testing you to see how you would handle a situation like this. Say, now, what would you tell the Sheriff's Office? He was supposed to have been at the county jail twenty minutes ago.

DEPUTY: I don't know, what am I supposed to tell them?

FRED: Well, you could call the dispatcher and tell him that your prisoner escaped somewhere off Highway 90.

DEPUTY: Now, what in the hell am I going to do that for? In the first place, we're not anywhere near Highway 90. In the second place, you had charge of the prisoner.

FRED: You're a jerk, do you know that? You're never gonna make it around this police department or any other police department. When a superior officer gives you an order you obey it!

DEPUTY: Look, first you told me you shot the man, then you told me you didn't. And then you told me something else. I don't know whether to believe you or not. But let me tell you something, I'm not going to lie for you or anybody else.

FRED: Okay. Go on, get out of here.

DEPUTY: I'll see you back at the County Jail, *Chief. (Deputy exits, goes to the stand.)*

HAROLD: Now then, Deputy Davis, if you were so certain that Chief Hall killed Danny Rosales, why didn't you arrest him right then and there?

DEPUTY: I couldn't find the body so I couldn't prove anything.

HAROLD: Did you actually see Fred Hall shoot Danny Rosales?

DEPUTY: No, but I heard . . .

HAROLD: You were two hundred yards away in your squad car. How did you know what was going on out there? Just answer yes or no. Did you see Hall shoot Rosales?

DEPUTY: No, sir.

HAROLD: One more question: were you granted immunity from prosecution by the State of Texas?

DEPUTY: Yes, sir, I was.

HAROLD: So, in return for this immunity you have agreed to come forward with the most damaging testimony you can think of to bury Fred Hall, isn't that right?

DEPUTY: No, sir, that's not right. The statement I made was written four months before I was granted immunity.

HAROLD: The District Attorney didn't come along at that time and tell you, "Now, if you behave and be a good boy and tell us what we want to hear, you won't get prosecuted," right?

DEPUTY: No, sir, that's not true. I made an oath at the very beginning to uphold the laws of the State of Texas. That's exactly what I told Mrs. Rosales when she came looking for her husband at the police station the night he was killed. *(Flashback.)*

BERTA: Deputy, where's my husband? They say they haven't seen him at the booking desk and it's way past midnight?

DEPUTY: I honestly don't know where he is, Mrs. Rosales.

BERTA: What do you mean? You arrested him two hours ago.

DEPUTY: Mrs. Rosales, there's nothing I can tell you right now, believe me. If any information comes in you'll be the first to know. Now, if you'll excuse me, there's some problems here at the jail, seems like there's a riot going on or something.

BERTA: You expect us to be treated like this? You arrest my husband and say you're going to take him to jail and he's nowhere to be found!

DEPUTY: Please, I'm trying to do everything I can to find out what happened to your husband.

BERTA: No you're not, what do you care? To you Danny is just another Mexican.

DEPUTY: That's not true, Mrs. Rosales. Less than a month ago I gave Danny a break, not because he was brown or green or any other color, but because I believed he'd live up to his word.

BERTA: Where's my husband? Is he hurt? Tell me where to look for him.

DEPUTY: Why don't you ask his *friend*, Kiki Ventura.

BERTA: I don't care about him, all I care about is what's happened to Danny.

DEPUTY: You better care. The only difference between Kiki and Judas is that Judas hung himself. But I promise you one thing, everybody's going to get what's coming to them, everybody.

DEBBIE: (*Back at the witness stand, Debbie has been sworn in and has begun her testimony.*) It was late, but Mama and I were sitting up talking . . . Mama, what are you doing up so late?

GRACE: Waiting for your father and reading the Good Book.

DEBBIE: Oh, how exciting.

GRACE: It is dear, it's the best-seller of all time.

DEBBIE: I thought "Gone with the Wind" was.

GRACE: Do you want to know what passage I was reading?

DEBBIE: Sure.

GRACE: 1 Corinthians 6:19. "Know ye not that your body is the temple of the Holy Spirit?"

DEBBIE: Oh, Mama, not again.

GRACE: The Bible says that thou shalt not defile the body with immorality. Debbie, does Stevie ever touch you?

DEBBIE: Of course he touches me, he touches me all the time.

GRACE: Debbie, you know what I mean. Does he touch you . . . you know, where he shouldn't?

DEBBIE: Of course not, I wouldn't let him touch me there.

GRACE: I know he kisses you good night, because I've seen the two of you on the front porch, but does he ever, I don't know how to say this . . . does he ever stick his tongue in your mouth!

DEBBIE: Oh, Mama! Of course not!

GRACE: I know you're a good girl, Debbie, I just want to make sure you save yourself for your wedding night.

DEBBIE: Mama, you know something, I just made up my mind this very night! There ain't gonna be no wedding!

GRACE: Debbie, you can't be serious. We told all our friends and relatives. (*A car pulls into the driveway, Grace reacts.*) Is that your Daddy and Steve?

DEBBIE: Stevie says he wants to start having lots of kids. Sometimes I think the only reason he wants to get married is so he can sleep with me!

GRACE: Debbie, don't say things like that. (*She is looking out the window. Steve runs into the house past Grace.*) Hello, Stevie dear.

STEVE: Hello, Mrs. Hall. (*He stands nervously by Debbie's side as she ignores him.*)

GRACE: (*Opening the screen door and going out to the driveway.*) Fred, what are you doing? Did you know there was another disturbance at the county jail? I heard it on the radio.

FRED: (*Sitting behind the wheel, exhausted.*) I can't go.

GRACE: Fred, what's the matter with you? Is your stomach bothering you again? (*She opens the car door.*) You've been working too hard. You're not going out again, are you?

FRED: Have to.

GRACE: Well, at least let me drive, scoot over. (*Noticing the body in the back.*) What's that! Another drunk?

STEVE: (*To Debbie, inside the house.*) Debbie, did a guy named Danny Rosales ever speak to you or anything?

DEBBIE: Yeah, sure, so what?

STEVE: Just answer my question.

DEBBIE: I sat with him once on the Greyhound to Dallas. He was kinda nice, uneducated, but nice.

STEVE: Did he ever touch you or try to make a pass at you or anything like that?

DEBBIE: Why are you asking me these questions? What are you, my father or what?!

STEVE: Debbie, your father just killed a man for no reason!

GRACE: (*Enter Fred, followed by Grace.*) Answer my questions? Where is the Deputy? What did you do, tell me? (*Fred sits, silent.*)

DEBBIE: Daddy, are you all right? You look so pale.

GRACE: Stevie, do you know what happened?

STEVE: Fred said it was an accident. I don't really know, I didn't see it.

GRACE: Fred, for the love of God, will you speak up and say something!

DEBBIE: Do you want me to get you your painkillers? (Fred nods his head "yes.")

GRACE: Debbie, pour your Daddy some coffee, he needs to think straight.

FRED: Get me a beer.

GRACE: No more drinking, Fred. Now tell me, why are you so worried? You said it was an accident.

FRED: Too many damn witnesses.

STEVE: I think I better go home. Goodnight, Debbie!

GRACE: Stevie Peters, you stay put. Let me tell you something about this family. We stick together, you hear? If you're going to be a part of us, you've got to stick with us come hell or high water, ya hear?

STEVE: Yes 'um.

FRED: Got to dispose of the body.

DEBBIE: Why don't you do what you always do, Daddy, take it to the funeral home.

FRED: I need a drink!

GRACE: I said, no more drinking! Now, listen to me, you and Stevie clean up the back seat of the car and put the body in the trunk. Hurry up, before it gets light.

FRED: You're right, you're right. Come on, Steve. (They exit.)

GRACE: Debbie?

DEBBIE: Yes, Mama.

GRACE: You'd do anything for your Daddy, wouldn't you dear?

DEBBIE: Of course, Mama.

GRACE: Your father is very sick, you know that, dear.

DEBBIE: From the shoot-out and the drugs and the liquor?

GRACE: That's right, dear, we have to protect him. Especially when he makes a mistake like tonight.

DEBBIE: What are we going to do, Mama?

GRACE: I think we're going to have to go for a little ride, dear, this very night.

DEBBIE: Can't it wait until morning, Mama, it's awful late?

GRACE: I'm afraid not, dear, you and I are going to have to help your Daddy get rid of that body.

DEBBIE: You and I, Mama? You and I?

STEVE: *(Re-entering.)* It's all done, we moved the body into the trunk and the Chief's hosing down the back seat. Can I go now, Mrs. Hall?

DEBBIE: Stevie, Mama needs somebody to help her . . . get rid of that body.

STEVE: No, I've done more than my share.

DEBBIE: Stevie, she wants me to go with her!

STEVE: Mrs. Hall, can't you just go to the county jail and tell them the truth? Fred's the Chief of Police, they'll protect him.

GRACE: No, there's a Mexican American riot going on there. This could have something to do with it.

STEVE: Well, I'm sorry. I just can't deal with this anymore, I just can't. *(Steve exits.)*

DEBBIE: Stevie! Stevie!

FRED: All done. What now?

GRACE: Fred, you tell me!

FRED: Don't know, can't think.

GRACE: The only place I could think of is my brother's ranch, in Carthage, by the Louisiana border.

FRED: Five hundred miles away?!

GRACE: Exactly, no one will ever find it there.

FRED: I'll clean up and get started.

GRACE: No, you stay here in case anybody comes looking for you.

DEBBIE: Daddy, she wants me to go with her.

FRED: Grace, I don't think this child . . .

GRACE: I need her to help me with the driving. You stay here and go to work in the morning as though nothing had happened. And call in sick for me at the bank.

FRED: I knew I could count on you, Grace. *(They embrace and kiss.)*

GRACE: I love you, Fred.

FRED: Take this .38 pistol and holster. *(Handing Grace his pistol and holster.)*

DEBBIE: I don't want to go!

GRACE: Hush up, girl! From now on we do what I say! *(They exit.)*

KIKI: *(Late at night.)* Hey, Berta, what are you doing out so late? Sabes qué, I got some money for Danny! Now he can pay off that farmer, here.

BERTA: Where did you get this money?

KIKI: My abuelita died and gave it to me.

BERTA: Does your abuelita wear a badge and carry a shotgun?

KIKI: What are you talking about, Berta?

BERTA: I thought you were Danny's friend.

KIKI: I am. I am his best friend.

BERTA: Then how could you lie to the police, how could you take their money?

KIKI: Hey, now, don't be accusing anybody of being a snitch. People can get hurt for less.

BERTA: Mentiroso! You told the police that Danny stole a new stereo and TV.

KIKI: That's a lie!

BERTA: And do you know where they took him? To the Old Alamo School Road. You know what they do to boys down there—they beat the hell out of them—and you helped them.

KIKI: Chingao, Berta. Is that what they did, lo llevaron allí? ¡Hijos de puta!

BERTA: What did you tell them about Danny?

KIKI: Nothing. The Sheriff was angry at me for making him wait four hours by the side of the road. All I said was that Danny had a new stereo and TV. I had to tell him *something.*

BERTA: ¡Madre de Dios!

KIKI: He wanted to get Danny, I don't know why. I just told him the first crazy thing that came to the top of my head. I swear, Berta, I didn't mean to hurt Danny. The Sheriff was going to beat me, he was going to throw me in jail.

BERTA: So you turned Danny in to take your place!

KIKI: I couldn't help it. They were going to send me away for a long time. Tú sabes, I have to survive, I live from day to day, sleeping in the back seat of my car half the time. I ain't got nothing, I never had nothing.

BERTA: Neither did Danny. But at least he was trying to go straight. I hate you! I hope you burn in hell! I wish you were dead!

KIKI: Berta, don't you see, I am dead! *(Exit.)*

DEBBIE: *(Back at the witness stand.)* It was the most horrible thing I had ever experienced in all my life. There we were, Mama and me, on the expressway in the middle of the morning rush hour with a dead body in the trunk! Neither of us had had much sleep. We didn't know what had caused the accident. Daddy was in a state of shock. He couldn't answer my mother's questions. She had always depended upon him for everything. The drive took six hours. I remember stopping along the way and buying some shovels and a digger. It was the month of September and it was still very hot in Texas.

GRACE: The sun is so bright today, like a blinding white disk.

DEBBIE: I ain't never seen so many dead animals on the road in all my life.

GRACE: Look how brown and dried the earth is.

DEBBIE: Just like that boy back there.

GRACE: There's the start of my brother's ranch, three hundred acres.

DEBBIE: Mama, what if somebody sees us?

GRACE: Don't worry, I used to play here when I was a little girl. I know a spot no one will ever find.

DEBBIE: I'm not going anywhere near that body!

GRACE: Debbie, I don't expect you to!

DEBBIE: How are you going to do it all by yourself?

GRACE: Simple. I'll back the car up near the space for the grave, wrap the rope around the body, loop it over a tree branch, and hoist it up out of the car trunk.

DEBBIE: How long do you think it's going to take to dig a grave in this hard clay earth?

GRACE: Don't you worry, I'll do all the digging.

DEBBIE: But Mother, why did you bring two shovels?

GRACE: (*Starting to dig the grave.*) After all this is over, we'll go up to our cabin at Lake Austin and relax.

DEBBIE: Mama, what happens to a man's spirit when he dies?

GRACE: Well, if he believes that Christ is the Saviour, then he'll be with Him. Honey, don't worry yourself about things like that. I know that you're thinking about that boy, but there's nothing we can do to bring him back to life. We have to think of the living.

DEBBIE: But Mama, there's too many witnesses! Even Daddy said so. Maybe we should just tell the truth.

GRACE: What is the truth?

DEBBIE: That it was an accident, that Daddy didn't mean to do it. Don't you see, we're just making matters worse by trying to cover it up. Why don't we just go to a police station and tell them the truth?

GRACE: Debbie, I got too many things on my mind to argue with you. Besides, the truth will come out in the end, it always does. Now then, I'm going to dig a small grave and conceal the body. This clay earth will protect it until such a time as we need to retrieve it. Hand me some of those plastic bags.

DEBBIE: What are you going to use them for?

GRACE: To cover up his face and chest and other portions of his body.

DEBBIE: What for?

GRACE: You don't want dirt falling on his face, do you? (*Blackout.*)

DEPUTY: (*With Berta at the front door of the Hall home.*) Fred. Fred! Mrs. Rosales wanted to talk to you and asked me to come along with her.

FRED: Well, good morning, Mrs. Rosales, what can I do for you?

BERTA: I want to know what you did to my husband.

FRED: Well, he's in a lot of trouble. Not only did he escape my custody, but he attempted to assault a law officer.

BERTA: That's a lie. If he had escaped, he would have gotten word to me.

FRED: Maybe he's out having a little drink with the boys.

BERTA: You beat him, didn't you? And then you shot him!

FRED: Mrs. Rosales, I think you'd better get off my property.

BERTA: What have you done to my husband?

FRED: The last time I saw him he was high-tailing it through the woods.

BERTA: Then how do you explain his shoe and the pool of dried blood I found near the side of the road?

FRED: Is that true, Davis?

DEPUTY: That's right, Fred, we spent all morning out there. There's dried blood and lots of it.

FRED: Well, that don't prove nothing. The gun did go off accidentally, I could have wounded him, but he ran off! Besides, there's no body, where's the body?

DEPUTY: Fred, I think you'd better come down to the station and answer some questions.

FRED: Yeah, sure, I got nothing to hide.

DEPUTY: One more thing, Fred, let's see your sawed-off shotgun. (*Blackout.*)

GRACE: (*Later on that after noon at Lake Austin.*) There, you see, we made it, safe and sound.

DEBBIE: It was such a *long* drive.

GRACE: Texas is a country all unto itself, darling.

DEBBIE: Who would have thought it would have taken six hours to dig that grave.

GRACE: You didn't get any blood on your clothes, did you?

DEBBIE: Only on my hands.

GRACE: Now then, we have one more little task to do and then we'll be all done.

DEBBIE: What now?

GRACE: The trunk. First we have to get rid of the shovels and digger. Then we have to scrub it down real good.

DEBBIE: Oh no, not again!

GRACE: We'll scrub it until it's clean as a whistle!

DEBBIE: Mama, I still don't understand why we're going through all of this. You say we have every intention of telling the truth, of going back there and uncovering the body and clearing Daddy's name! Why are we here in Lake Austin hiding from everybody?

GRACE: We're not hiding! (*She opens the trunk and takes out the shovels.*) We're just waiting until your father can get his wits back together again and explain this unfortunate incident.

DEBBIE: Mother, I'm going to be sick.

GRACE: Hand me the cleaning detergent and that towel. (*As she pulls out a plastic bag.*)

DEBBIE: What's in there!

GRACE: Just some garbage left over from the picnic last weekend.

DEPUTY: (*Entering rather suddenly.*) Excuse me, are you Mrs. Grace Hall?

GRACE: Oh, my goodness, you startled me! Why, yes, I am, is something the matter, officer?

DEPUTY: Are you Debbie Hall?

DEBBIE: No, I'm Berta Rosales.

GRACE: Debbie! These children have no respect nowadays.

DEPUTY: Mind if I take a look at the inside of your trunk?

GRACE: Why, what ever are you looking for?

DEPUTY: Two shovels and digger. (*Commenting on the tools.*) God, what is that awful smell?

GRACE: Well, you see, officer, we just got done burying an old dog of ours.

DEBBIE: That's right, and his name was Danny Rosales. Only, you know something, we couldn't get his eyes closed! (*Blackout.*)

JUDGE: (*Back at the trial.*) Ladies and gentlemen of the jury, before we begin the closing arguments, I want to remind you once more that this is a two-stage trial and that your first task is to decide on the guilt or innocence of the defendant. Your second task is to assess the punishment. Now, for the first stage you can find the defendant, Fred Hall, (1) guilty of murder in the first degree, or (2) guilty of aggravated assault, or (3) not guilty as charged. Proceed with the closing arguments.

ROWENA: Ladies and gentlemen, this is more than just another case of murder in a small Texas town. This is a trial with international repercussions. What is being tried here is the American system of justice and whether or not all the people have the inalienable rights promised to them by the Constitution of the United States.

HAROLD: Ladies and gentlemen of the jury, Ms. Saldivar would have us believe that the American judicial system is on trial here. That is not the case, what is on trial here is whether or not an officer of the law has the right to defend himself under attack.

ROWENA: On the eve of my involvement in this case, I reaffirmed my professional commitment not to identify too closely with my client, a rule which we were taught in law school. But the violent manner in which Danny Rosales died tore away the veil of my impartiality.

HAROLD: The prosecutor has admitted being blinded by her emotional involvement in this case. Consequently, she has turned this trial into an arena for her political crusading. But she will find no scapegoat here, no sacrifice to appease the masses.

ROWENA: Danny Rosales was accused of a crime he did not commit, arrested in his home, beaten without cause in his driveway, dragged into the woods, beaten again, and then shot to death at point-blank range by the highest ranking law enforcement officer of the town in which he lived. If this could happen to Danny Rosales, it could happen to me or even to you.

HAROLD: If my client is guilty of anything, he is guilty of being overzealous in his dedication to duty; a man who served his country for thirty years in the United States Air Force, a God-fearing family man who almost gave up his life three years ago in an exchange of gunfire with three suspects in a liquor store. And yet the prosecution paints him as a sadistic racist.

ROWENA: Ladies and gentlemen, if you decide in your wisdom that this was not first degree murder, which I most certainly think it was, then surely Fred Hall can be found guilty of nothing less than aggravated assault in which he caused the death of Danny Rosales through his negligence. According to the coroner's report, the sawed-off double barreled LeFever shotgun was no more than three and a half feet from the point of impact and wadding from the shell was found imbedded in Danny's chest. Was this negligence? No, this was an execution-style murder.

HAROLD: Let us examine what happened that night. While there is no denying that Fred Hall was carrying a shotgun when he arrested Danny Rosales, there is also no denying that Rosales attacked Hall. There was a struggle; Rosales grabbed the shotgun with both hands, kicked Hall to the ground, and while attempting to seize the weapon, it discharged, accidentally. It was self-defense, not murder.

ROWENA: Now we come to the gruesome cover-up attempt. And please keep in mind that by your actions today, tomorrow we will judge those who helped Fred Hall cover up the crime. How could this so-called devoted father and husband allow his wife and daughter to become involved in this macabre affair? And to those of you who say that Fred Hall was temporarily out of his mind, I say, he—with the help of his wife—coldly and calculatingly tried to hide the deed by disposing of the evidence 400 miles from the scene of the crime.

HAROLD: Ladies and gentlemen, if Fred Hall was going to go out there and kill somebody on purpose, do you think he would take this boy who was going to be his son-in-law to witness a killing? Does that make any sense?

ROWENA: Why was Danny Rosales killed? Was it because he was born poor? Was it because he had been caught stealing in the past? Was it because he was too proud to confess to a crime he did not commit? Or was it because he was a Mexican?

HAROLD: Race had nothing to do with this! We give our police officers the right to bear arms. How can we expect them to perform their duties properly if they are brought to trial each and every time there is a confrontation with a common criminal? It is time that we stopped coddling and indulging the criminals and started caring more about the police officers.

ROWENA: But does a badge and uniform give a man the license to kill?

HAROLD: Examine your hearts and find the only possible verdict in this case. Not guilty!

ROWENA: Guilty of first degree murder!

JUDGE: Now then, ladies and gentlemen of the jury, have you arrived at a verdict? Will you please hand it to the Bailiff. (*They do so.*) What is the ruling?

BAILIFF: The jury finds the defendant, Fred Hall, guilty of aggravated assault.

BERTA: Of aggravated assault! Rowena?

ROWENA: It means that Hall caused Danny's death, but it is a term usually associated with traffic accidents.

BERTA: Traffic accidents?

JUDGE: We have now reached the second point of the trial, which is where you, the jury, deliberate and decide upon the appropriate punishment that should be assessed in this case. Counselors will make their final statements.

ROWENA: Ladies and gentlemen, it is not our place to question the wisdom that you have used in arriving at a verdict of guilty of aggravated assault. But I think that the situation in general cries out for punishment in this case and the punishment you have found the defendant guilty of is two-to-ten years in prison. Now, the defense has filed a motion asking that you consider probation for the defendant. This would be like letting Fred Hall go free for the killing of Danny Rosales. Mr. Pearl made the statement that the law allows a man like Mr. Hall to carry a twelve-gauge sawed-off shotgun. That is true, but along with that privilege comes the responsibility to use it with discretion and extreme caution. There is a saying, originally in Latin, that goes, "Who will guard the guards?" I am talking about guards who could preserve any type of oppression they care to. Who will guard your liberty and mine? I think your verdict should speak to that question. Do not probate the sentence of two-to-ten years. Probation is no punishment and without punishment we have no protection. That is our system of justice.

HAROLD: May it please the court, ladies and gentlemen of the jury, the verdict at which you arrived was probably a very just one. You felt that the gun was not handled properly and that it caused the death of a man. That is now history. When I was selecting you, I told you that the defense was going to be looking for the God-like qualities in you. We are created in God's image and we are the only creatures that have the ability to show mercy and compassion, just as God is merciful and compassionate. No matter what we do here today, we cannot bring life back to Danny Rosales. Please, we have heard one terrible tragedy, don't cap it with another. Please, for your sake, don't let another tragedy occur. Each and every one of us has to look at ourselves in the mirror each morning. Make sure what you do here today you can be proud of tomorrow, when you look in that mirror. Fred Hall is a man of good reputation who has never been convicted of a felony, nor has he ever been given probation. I urge you to probate him. Thank you.

JUDGE: Ladies and gentlemen of the jury, have you arrived at a verdict?

BAILIFF: They have, your Honor.

JUDGE: Hand it to the Bailiff, please. I will read the verdict. "The Jury, having found the defendant, Fred Hall, guilty of the offense of aggravated assault, a third degree felony, assesses the defendant's punishment as confinement in the Texas Department of Corrections for a period of not less than two nor more than ten years."

BERTA: What happens now, Rowena? (*The Hall family is congratulating themselves upon hearing the verdict.*)

HAROLD: (*Walking over to Rowena.*) Congratulations, counselor.

ROWENA: For what?

HAROLD: For winning the case. My client was found guilty.

ROWENA: You know damn well that with time off for good behavior he could be out in twenty months.

HAROLD: True, but he's still going to serve some time. Look, why don't we go have a drink afterwards and talk about the case?

ROWENA: No thanks, I'm going to be too busy filing for a Department of Justice investigation into this case!

HAROLD: Miss Saldivar, you know you can't try a man twice for the same crime.

ROWENA: But you can try a man for violating another man's civil rights.

HAROLD: Don't waste your time, counselor, don't waste your time. (*Exits.*)

BERTA: Civil rights? What does that mean, Rowena? What about his life, can they bring back his life?

ROWENA: Berta, listen to me, we're not through yet, we're going to fight this all the way. Protests, letters to Congress, appeals, radio and television fund drives . . .

BERTA: I don't care what you do, Rowena, I've had it with the courts and the police and the Gringos! Rowena, crees que todavía estás en law school? This is Texas, not Harvard! There is no justice for Chicanos here! (*Exits.*)

DEPUTY: Miss Saldivar.

ROWENA: Yes, Deputy.

DEPUTY: Did you hear? Grace Hall pleaded no contest to the charge of concealing physical evidence. She was fined $49.50 in court costs.

ROWENA: $49.50! If Danny weighed 154 pounds at the time of his death, that means she got off with about thirty cents a pound!

DEBBIE: Stevie and I are getting married next Saturday.

BERTA: They killed my husband many times.

DEBBIE: All my family and friends will be at the wedding.

BERTA: Once when he was born poor.

DEBBIE: A country and western band will be playing.

BERTA: Once when he didn't get a decent education.

DEBBIE: We'll have fajitas and kegs of Lone Star beer.

BERTA: Once with a shotgun at the Old Alamo School Road.

DEBBIE: We're going to Las Vegas for our honeymoon.

BERTA: Once with a pick and shovel near the Louisiana border.

DEBBIE: We plan to have lots of kids.

BERTA: And once in a court of law.

DEBBIE: I'll be dressed in white.

BERTA: I'll be dressed in black.

ROWENA: In 1977, two years after Danny Rosales' death, we realized a great victory. Fred and Grace Hall were indicted by a federal grand jury. They were eventually found guilty of violating Danny Rosales' civil rights. Fred Hall was sentenced to life in prison, and Grace Hall was sentenced to three years in prison. But was this such a great victory? Did you hear what happened in Mejia, Texas, a couple of years ago? Three black men drowned while in police custody. And just last year in San Antonio they shot Héctor Santoscoy and . . .

Rancho Hollywood
"A California Dream"

CHARACTERS

GOVERNOR RIO RICO, *the last Mexican Governor of California, a middle-aged mulatto or Mexican man.*
DOÑA VICTORIA RICO, *the Governor's fair-skinned "Spanish" wife.*
RAMONA RICO, *the Ricos' young daughter, a brown mestiza.*
JEDEDIAH GOLDBANGER SMITH, *a Yankee trader-trapper-gold-miner-soldier-capitalist with a vision.*
TONTA GERONIMA SINMUHOW, *an Indian maid, maiden.*
YALLER MARCUS MALCOM KUNTA KINTE, *a high yaller slave, worker, invisible man.*

Place: *Los Angeles, California*
Time: *1840s to the present*

ACT I

At rise the Director is assisted by his cameraman as they shoot a movie entitled "Ye Olde California Days." The principals are off stage preparing themselves for their entrance: Ramona, an ingenue, fiery Latina type; Joaquín, a young man dressed as a peon; Sinmuhow, a Native American woman; Victoria, an older matronly type, Spanish looking; and Rico, a dark debonair older Mexican male.

DIRECTOR: *(To his cameraman.)* If everybody's here, let's shoot the balcony scene. *(Noises backstage, people talking.)*

CAMERAMAN: Attention everybody! Quiet on the set.

DIRECTOR: The fiery impetuous Ramona *(Enter Ramona.)* is pacing nervously on her balcony waiting for her demon lover, Cisco. Stamp your feet, clap your hands, say your line! A medium shot here, camera.

RAMONA: Oh no, this cannot go on. Where is my sultry Cisco? I want him to take me away to the Rancho Grande of ecstasy!

DIRECTOR: That's good, Ronnie, but I need more of an accent. Say "dis" instead of "this" and "wan" instead of "want." And throw in a few "olés." Zoom in on a close-up on "olé."

RAMONA: Dis cun nut go on. I wan heem to take me away. Olé!

DIRECTOR: Wonderful! I love it! Remember, this is nineteenth-century California, just before the Gold Rush, when all those gay caballeros and sexy señoritas were dancing fandangos until dawn. Now then, what's missing?

CAMERAMAN: You forgot the peon.

DIRECTOR: Of course, where is my sleepy peon? *(Enter Joaquín.)* There you are. Oh, I love your outfit, it's so . . . I don't know . . . native. What's your name?

JOAQUIN: Joaquín.

DIRECTOR: Walking?

JOAQUIN: No, Joaquín. Like in Joaquín Valley.

DIRECTOR: Mind if I call you Jack? Up against that wall. Now squat. *(Placing a sombrero that covers up his face.)* There!

JOAQUIN: Do I have any lines?

DIRECTOR: Lines!

CAMERAMAN: No lines.

DIRECTOR: Sorry, Jack. Move your sombrero a bit from time to time so we know you're not a statue. Who's next?

CAMERAMAN: The passerby. A lady of the night.

SINMUHOW: I am Sinmuhow. *(Entering.)*

DIRECTOR: Oh, you're Native American. Look everybody, a real honest to goodness Indian! We're going to have such good karma! *(He hugs her.)* Now then, this part calls for a Mexican, but I'm sure you can pass. At the very start of the scene you walk on undulating your hips like so. *(He walks across the set undulating his hips.)*

JOAQUIN: Yes, and that's my cue. I lift the brim of my sombrero, stick out my tongue, and pant.

DIRECTOR: Good. *(To cameraman).* Couldn't we put some fruit on her head? You know, then she could do the cha-cha-cha.

CAMERAMAN: That's old hat.

DIRECTOR: All right, forget it. Who's next?

CAMERAMAN: Victoria the maid. *(Enter Victoria.)*

VICTORIA: I was under the impression I was supposed to be her mother.

DIRECTOR: You are, dear, but you're also the maid. Aren't all mothers? Johnny, what is she supposed to be doing?

CAMERAMAN: *(Reading script.)* It says here, "enter making a tamale."

DIRECTOR: Oh, how ethnic. Well, where's your tamale? You little hot tamale you! *(Laughing at his own joke.)* Cut to a long shot.

VICTORIA: *(Pulling out a fake tamale.)* Ay, que ridículo.

DIRECTOR: Great! You speak Spanish! Throw in a few words every once in a while. Doesn't matter what you say, just as long as it sounds good. Give me your line.

VICTORIA: Ay Ramona, forget that no count Cisco, he is no good for you!

DIRECTOR: More accent!

RAMONA: Ay Mamá, I lub heem, he sets my heart on fi-errrrr.

DIRECTOR: What happens then?

CAMERAMAN: Her debonair, slightly-greying Spanish grandee father enters cracking his whip and drinking tequila.

DIRECTOR: Father! Father! Where's the Father?

RICO: Ay voy, I'm coming!

DIRECTOR: These people! *(To Cameraman who nods in agreement.)* You'd think this was the land of manana! *(Joaquín gets up to stretch.)*

VICTORIA: He's here!

RICO: Excuse me, I was getting made up. *(He enters with an excess of white powder on his face. The Director does not really see him.)*

DIRECTOR: Let's go! We have a tight schedule! I'm going to have to be a bitch about this!

CAMERAMAN: Places! Places! *(Joaquín squats back into place.)* Quiet! Quiet on the set! Ye Olde California Days, take one.

DIRECTOR: Lights! Camera! Wait. *(He runs up and places a plastic rose between Ramona's teeth.)* Action! *(The Lady of the Night strolls by dancing salsa. The Peon lifts up the brim of his sombrero and starts panting, grabbing his groin.)*

RAMONA: *(Stamping her feet and clapping her hands.)* Olé! O, dis can nut go on. Wear es my sultry Cisco? ı wan heem to take me to El Rancho Grande of Ecstasy!

VICTORIA: *(She drops her tamale as she enters.)* Ramona, forget dat no count Cisco, he es no goot for you.

RAMONA: Ay Mamá! You dropped your tamale. But I love heem, he puts my hard on fi-eerrrr.

VICTORIA: Well, put de fi-errrrr out! He es un bandido, un desesperado! If your Papá finds out he weeel keeel you!

RICO: *(Enter cracking his whip and drinking tequila from a bottle.)* Andale! Andale! Arriba! Arriba! *(Like Speedy González, like Trini López trilling and shouting.)* Ajúa! Trlllllingg!

DIRECTOR: Cut! Cut! *(To Cameraman.)* Has Central Casting gone color blind! I asked for a white Spanish grandee and they give me a dark farmworker!

VICTORIA: ¡Qué insulto!

RICO: Por eso me tardé tanto. Me pusieron todo este polvo.

DIRECTOR: Hey, no offense fellah, but you don't look very Spanish. You're supposed to be Ramona's father, the Spanish grandee.

RICO: Sir, I don't understand, even if I am as dark as a Moor, I could still be Ramona's father.

VICTORIA: That's right, Ramona is a mestiza.

DIRECTOR: A what?

VICTORIA: A mestiza. Half and half. If I, as her mother, am fair, and the father is dark, then the child is like café con leche.

RAMONA: I've never been described that way before.

VICTORIA: Yes, but that is what the Mexican people are, a mixture of Spanish and Indian.

RICO: And Arab and Jewish and African. . . .

DIRECTOR: That is very quaint, that is very informative. But this film is supposed to be about the Spanish Californios!

RICO: Mr. Director, with all due respect, I am afraid you have little conception of the Californio reality. The people of that time were

Mexican, not Spanish.

RAMONA: Jed, honey, listen to these people, they're trying to tell you something.

CAMERAMAN: It says here in the script that Ramona's father is "a Spanish grandee type, representative of the early aristocratic Californios."

RICO: But did you know that many of the founding families of the City of Los Angeles were black? The last Mexican Governor of California was a mulatto. His name was Pio Pico.

RAMONA: Who told you that?

RICO: I read it in a history book. They showed photos of him.

VICTORIA: That's right. All that stuff about the Spanish is pure bunk!

RICO: Look, I'm sure if you approached this film a bit more realistically, by doing some research, you'd find I could do this part.

DIRECTOR: All right! Have you all had your little says now? If you people ever want to work in this town again, you'll play your parts exactly the way I tell you to. Or you will never work anywhere in Hollywood again! Let's go! (He exits followed by the Cameraman.)

RICO: Oh, damn it! Now I did it!

JOAQUIN: Listen, I agree with you 100%. I'm sick and tired of playing these demeaning roles.

SINMUHOW: Me too, but I'm also sick and tired of car hopping at the Red-E-Go Drive-In.

RAMONA: I'll try and talk to him. Maybe I can cool him down a bit. (Exits.)

VICTORIA: (To Rico.) You did right in speaking out. Are you well versed in the California days? Oh, those must have been wonderful times, halcyon days. (The lights fade, except for a spot on Rico and Victoria. An old waltz from the period starts to play.)

RICO: I saw an old photo of the governor's wife. She looked like you, very fair, very Spanish.

VICTORIA: They must have been very happy, before the Gringos came.

RICO: (At this point Rico and Victoria are dancing a waltz downstage. Another spotlight shines upstage to reveal Joaquín and Ramona in an embrace bidding adieu.) Yes, but they were living on borrowed time. They had barely gained independence from Spain and secularized the missions when other problems arose.

VICTORIA: What could have possibly shattered such an idyllic dream?

RICO: The Indians, for one thing. (As Rico says this Tonta enters and *puts her head to the keyhole to eavesdrop.)* They were becoming increasingly bolder, attacking settlements, running away with livestock, killing our people.

VICTORIA: That would be solved in time. We would all become one race!

RICO: Perhaps, but then there was the constant bickering between those of us in the North and those from the South. *(Rico sees Joaquín and goes for him. Exit Joaquín and Tonta. A door slams.)* That young man is not to darken this door again!

VICTORIA: Don't get upset, dear, I was chaperoning them.

RICO: I don't care, he is not to set foot in this house again!

RAMONA: Why do you dislike Joaquín so much? Aside from the fact he is from the North?

RICO: I'll tell you why. He drinks, swears, reads suggestive books, shoots his pistols in the air, duels and plots insurrections. Is that enough?!

VICTORIA: *(Aside to Ramona.)* Just like your father did when he was young.

RAMONA: Good God in heaven!

RICO: And there she goes, using the name of God in vain again!

RAMONA: Why don't you admit the real reason you dislike him is because he is in the forefront of steering a new and independent course for us Californios.

RICO: There she goes, using that word again—Californio!

VICTORIA: But Rico, it's just a word the young people use to describe themselves nowadays.

RICO: Not good enough to call themselves Mexicanos como sus padres.

VICTORIA: Don't you remember we used to call ourselves "Criollos" to distinguish us from the Españoles?

RICO: That was yesterday. Today we are Mexican. And we shall always remain Mexican. To call ourselves anything else is treason. I am the Governor of this territory and I refuse to hear that word in my house!

VICTORIA: You are as unbending as a mountain; no wonder all the youth are rebelling.

RAMONA: There's some other reason why Papá hates Joaquín so much. Why don't you come out with it!

RICO: Mira, mira! Don't speak to me in that tone of voice. For one thing, his people are barely gente de razón. They are but one generation removed from the savages.

55

RAMONA: Papá, with all due respect, you claim to dislike Joaquín because of his lower class origins, yet mother tells me your grandparents were poor shepherds of the humblest class. (*Victoria is making frantic gestures and shaking her head "no."*)

RICO: So, your aristocratic mother, descendant of the conquistadores, told you that, eh?

VICTORIA: Your father comes from good stock, dear, good sound stock.

RICO: Yes, there's no comparison between myself and that young rogue. Why, he's practically a coyote, a half breed.

RAMONA: You're calling him a coyote! What are you? What am I?

VICTORIA: Ramona, show your father more respect!

RAMONA: I see now, you dislike him because he is not "Spanish."

RICO: He's also the black sheep of the family, he is, esa bola de indios . . .

RAMONA: Well, let me tell you something, that "indio" asked me to marry him and I said "yes!"

VICTORIA: Why Ramona, how improper! You know that the parents have to be consulted before a girl receives a proposal of marriage!

RICO: You will do no such thing!

RAMONA: Yes I will!

RICO: Get me a switch! I will beat her within a very inch of her life! Listen to me, young lady, you will marry only within your own class! You will marry someone of pure Spanish blood.

RAMONA: What difference does it make! You're not Spanish, I'm not Spanish!

RICO: Yes you are. Call yourself anything else and no gentleman will ever ask for your hand in marriage. Ramona, you don't know prejudice like we do.

VICTORIA: Listen to your father, he means well.

RICO: When I married your mother in Mexico City, her relatives looked down on her because I looked like a Moor!

VICTORIA: It's true, hija, that's why we came back to California.

RICO: I don't want the same thing happening to you!

RAMONA: My God, this is so confusing! Papá, don't you see, you're being a hypocrite!

RICO: (*Raising his hand to slap her. Victoria restrains him.*) Why can't you be like the little girl I once knew, who used to sit on my knee and listen to stories of why the sea is so salty, or why the full moon has the face of a rabbit.

RAMONA: I don't want to hear any more stories!

RICO: I used to tell her the reason people got dark is because they drank too much chocolate. But you're right, those days are past. Still, I have the final word in this house. You shall not see Joaquín again. I shall banish him to the farthest corners of this territory.

RAMONA: Nooooooooo! *(Ramona exits defiantly.)* We shall elope!

RICO: *(Trying to go after her.)* Ramona! Come back here!

VICTORIA: Let her go, give her time to cool her heels. You know, even if she marries the whitest man in California, if you can find one, their children could still be as dark as you. You never told her your grandmother was a mulatto, did you? *(Tonta reenters the scene and listens.)*

RICO: Why trouble our daughter with inconsequential matters concerning my lineage?

VICTORIA: Not so inconsequential when she has to explain to her husband why the child looks like the Queen of Sheba.

RICO: Listen here, woman, don't make fun of me!

VICTORIA: Rico . . .

RICO: I never denied my origins. My grandmother may have been a mulatto but my parents were mestizos. I, in turn, have become a gente de razón, a citizen with all the rights and benefits thereof.

VICTORIA: Where else but California could you begin life as a Negro and end up as an Español?

RICO: Listen to me! I have heard of places where one drop, just one little drop of black blood automatically makes you a slave, what they call a "nigger." I may have some black blood in me, but I am no slave.

VICTORIA: No Señor, you are not a slave. *(She embraces him.)*

TONTA: *(Rushing in.)* Señores! Señores! The Yankee Clipper ship has been sighted in the harbor!

VICTORIA: Oh, Rico, let's go down to the wharf and get our pick of things before the others!

RICO: Now you know why we're getting into debt! But it's too late, we'll go in the morning.

VICTORIA: I have a better idea. Why don't we invite the Captain for dinner? We'll have a light supper and then maybe a small baile afterwards.

RICO: *(As they walk away.)* My dear, it is precisely this ostentatious style of living which will be the ruin of us.

TONTA: *(Aside.)* A mulatto, his grandmother. I knew it! That wooly headed old vieja was as black as Cleopatra!

DIRECTOR: (*Breaking up the scene.*) I've been watching it all. I love it!

RAMONA: (*By his side.*) So you see, Jed, they were real people with real problems.

CAMERAMAN: I'm concerned about the father; he's somewhat of a racist.

DIRECTOR: Exactly! Exactly!

RICO: (*Re-entering.*) It's something that the Mexican people would work out in time. Don't you see, they *talked* about it.

DIRECTOR: You know, we could do a California "West Side Story." What happens next?

RICO: The Anglos came. Some hiked in over the mountains, others sailed in on the clipper ships.

TONTA: They brought their slaves.

DIRECTOR: We could get O. J. Simpson to play the slave. Now we need a big name star for the, uh, Captain of the clipper ship. Someone with charisma, poise, good looks . . . I got it! I got it!

CAMERAMAN: Got what?

DIRECTOR: I'll play the part. (*The cameraman groans.*) You play my slave. Where are we? Where are we? (*The other actors disperse, leaving the Director and Cameraman to set up the next scene.*)

CAMERAMAN: On a boat. Out in the harbor.

DIRECTOR: Oh, I love this. It's so Brechtian. What am I doing?

CAMERAMAN: You could be singing . . . a popular song of the day.

JED: (*Becoming Jedediah Smith.*) "Oh Susana, oh don't you cry for me . . . for I'm bound to Californee with my banjo on my knee."

RUFUS: (*Turning into the Slave.*) Land, Massa Jed, land!

JED: There she is, Rufus, Californee! Ain't she purty! The Spanish thought it was an island inhabited by a tribe of Amazons.

RUFUS: What's a Amazons?

JED: Warrior women, Rufus, who wore breastplates of solid gold and slew every man in their path. Their queen was named Calafia. So they named the island California. She was reputed to be a black woman.

RUFUS: Land sakes! What was a nigger woman doing out here?

JED: It was only myth, Rufus, mere fantasy. But the cursed reality is that Spanish is the language spoken here, so let's get on with our Spanish lesson. "Fina tela aquí!"

RUFUS: Fina tela aquí . . . what I say?

JED: Fine cloth here! Now, repeat after me. "Mercancías, muebles!"

RUFUS: Mercancías! Muebles! That means merchandise, furniture.

JED: Fine. Now, here's a very important phrase: "Bajas intereses de crédito."

RUFUS: Bajas intereses de crédito!

JED: Good. That means "low interest rates." Californios love buying on credit. They are all show. So put the bright colors up front and hide the drab ones in the back. And never take your eyes off of them! They'll steal you blind.

RUFUS: Just like you, eh Massa Jed?

JED: (Holding up a shoe.) Lookee here, do you know what this is?

RUFUS: Looks like a shoe to me.

JED: This here's money, boy, money. They're called California Banknotes. Mexicans pay in rawhide, which we turn into shoes and sell it back to them.

RUFUS: Why don't they make their own shoes?

JED: Shhhh! Don't say that! They lazy, boy, they stupid. They depend almost entirely on us Yankee clipper ships.

RUFUS: Shoot! We gots the market cornered.

JED: Ya dang right!

RICO: We gonna make *us* a pile of money!

JED: *Me* a pile of money.

RUFUS: You a pile.

JED: Now then, if you're going to sell to these people you have to understand them. Let me read you a passage from a book written in 1840 by Richard Henry Dana called "Two Years Before the Mast." (Clearing his throat and reading.) "The Californio men are generally indolent . . ."

RUFUS: What's a insolent? (Reading over his shoulder.)

JED: That's "indolent" with a "d." It means lazy. (Reading again.) "The men are of a harmless disposition, fond of spiritous liquors, who care little for the welfare of their children. The women have but little virtue, the jealousy of their men is extreme, and the revenge deadly and almost certain." Now, what does that tell you about the Californios?

RUFUS: Whew! Don't mess wit de women folk! And, uh, some of dat dere sound what you said I is, 'specially de parts 'bout liquor and indolent.

JED: (Pulling out a flask.) Ain't nothing wrong with having a little drink now and then. Now then, what else you want to know about greasers? I read about 'em in all these books here.

RUFUS: Why you call 'em greasers?

JED: 'Cause they got greasy hair and they eat greasy food. *(Jed combs his greasy hair.)* You see, Rufus, there's very few white people in the country. The Californios are a mixture of Spanish and bloody Aztec!

RUFUS: Bloody Aztec!

JED: That's right. The bloody Aztecs used to practice human sacrifice and rip the hearts out of their victims' chests. Then they made sandwiches out of the hearts and sold them on streetcorners. That's why you have to be careful what you eat down here or you're liable to come down with Moctezuma's revenge!

RUFUS: Must have been a white man who wrote that.

JED: So, figure them out and skin them alive! And if you make me enough money on this trip . . . I'll make you a free man!

RUFUS: *(Pulling out a contract.)* You put that in writing!

JED: Hey! You're not supposed to know how to read . . . or write, you sneaky coon, you!

RUFUS: Sign! *(They shake on it. Blackout. Voices heard backstage. Spot on Tonta shown preparing herself for the next scene.)*

DIRECTOR: *(Voice offstage.)* What's the next scene? Where are we?

CAMERAMAN: Back at the Rancho. The gay Californios are preparing for the night's festivities. *(Voice offstage.)*

TONTA: Californios didn't prepare anything. We servants did it all. *(Entering.)*

DIRECTOR: Okay, Okay. Pretend you're making tortillas or something. And, uh, talk to yourself, complaining.

TONTA: *(Improvising.)* Pinche gente! Puras parrandas! They have to have a fandango every night. Why they hardly pause for an earthquake and continue right on dancing when it stops! *(Tonta stops, hears voice off to the side, sees Joaquín and Ramona entering the garden, stops to listen.)*

RAMONA: Joaquín! I'm so glad you're here, querido!

JOAQUIN: Your father has banished me to a military outpost in Sonoma.

RAMONA: Take me with you, I will go with you this very night!

JOAQUIN: Out of the question. It's too dangerous. Russians to the north, Yankees to the east, British pirates.

RAMONA: Well, then we'll leave the country. We'll go to Mexico or Europe. Someplace where we can be together.

JOAQUIN: I will never leave California. It is my home.

RAMONA: Well then . . . Joaquín, I thought we were going to elope tonight. I even packed my bags!

JOAQUIN: Ramona, mi amor, we must respect your father's wishes. I will work very hard and rise up through the ranks. I will repell the invaders from our land. Then he will respect me.

RAMONA: He will never respect you, Joaquín. You see, my father dislikes you because of your skin color, because you look like an indio.

JOAQUIN: Ramona, how can you say such a thing about your father? That's preposterous! Your father may be an old crustacean because of his politics, but a bigot he is not.

RAMONA: Joaquín, I'm speaking the truth. Listen to me, we must leave him and start our own lives. *(Tonta starts walking towards them.)*

JOAQUIN: Shhh, someone is coming. I must go! Promise you'll wait for me!

RAMONA: Yes, I will, of course, but don't you see . . . my father will never have anything to do with you because you are not Spanish.

JOAQUIN: Shhh, not another word. We are all the same raza. We will work things out. We always have before. *(He starts to leave but rushes back to Ramona.)* ¡Ay Ramona, no voy a poder vivir sin ti! *(He turns to go and crashes into Tonta.)*

TONTA: Oye! If Don Rico sees you he'll make chorizo out of you!

JOAQUIN: I'm leaving! I'm leaving! Querida, adiós. *(Joaquín hears footsteps coming in the direction of his exit.)* Who's that? One of the guests?

TONTA: By the sound of the footsteps it is Don Rico himself! He's probably loading his revolver!

RAMONA: Quick! Hide! My parents are coming! *(Joaquín makes desperate motions.)* Behind the pillar, under the table, anywhere! *(Depending upon the set Joaquín can become a statue, lamp, fountain, etc.)* Tonta, cover for us, please!

TONTA: Why should I? You live in a dream world. Your life is full of intrigues and little masquerades. But who do you think get's stuck with all the mierda?

RAMONA: Tonta, ¡por favor! *(Ramona sees that Joaquín has tried to turn into a statue. She grabs him and exits opposite Rico and Victoria's entrance.)*

RICO: *(Entering.)* Who were you talking to?

TONTA: Nobody. You know me. I'm a little loca. Sometimes I talk to myself.

VICTORIA: *(Who was not fooled.)* Tonta, be sure to prepare a room for the Captain of the Yankee clipper ship. He may stay the night.

TONTA: Shall I leave the pile of loose change in a bowl in his room as customary?

RICO: Yes, yes, of course. Show him some of that famous Californio hospitality!

VICTORIA: But I thought we were in debt!

RICO: Oh, this is just small change. Tonta, call my daughter to the living room. I want her to dance for our guests.

TONTA: Sí, Señor.

RICO: Ah, I see that my guests have arrived. (*Rico goes off into the wing and welcomes the guests in the next room.*)

VICTORIA: (*Taking Tonta aside.*) What did they say? (*While Victoria and Tonta are talking in private to the side, Ramona enters with Joaquín dressed in a ludicrous disguise. They kiss, he exits.*)

RICO: (*Voice offstage.*) Welcome! Welcome all to Rancho Madera Acebo! (*Music starts playing, Rico enters on stage.*) Ah, Ramona, there you are. I'm glad to see that your spirits have lifted. Come dear, dance for our guests. (*Applause is heard, shouting.*)

RAMONA: Oh no, Papá, please!

RICO: Yes, you will! (*Lights out except for spot on Ramona. She dances with the audience being the guests. Taped music.*)

EL BORREGO

Señora, su borreguito
Me quiere llevar al río
Y yo le digo que no,
Porque me muero de frío

Sale la linda
Sale la fea
Y el borreguito
Con su salea
Sale el negrito
Con su garrote
Y el borreguito
Con su salea

Tope que tope
Tope con ella
Tope que tope
Tope con él

(*Somewhere towards the end, Jed and Rufus enter, interrupting the party. Lights on. All stare at Jed.*)

JED: Excuse me, Señores, I didn't mean to interrupt your party.

RICO: ¡Bienvenidos! Yo soy el Gobernador Don Río Rico, para servirle.

RAMONA: My father, Don Río Rico, Governor of California, welcomes you!

RICO: ¡Mi casa es su casa!

JED: Why thank you, I think I'm going to like this casa very much.

RUFUS: (As Jed eyes Ramona.) Massa Jed, you be careful wit dem hot tamales. Did you notice the Gubnur? He's a darky!

JED: (Motioning to Rufus.) Damas y caballeros, I bringo you unos presentos! (Handing Rico a six pack of beer.) Cerveza for you! Coors! Best beer in the Westo. Decado del Hispánico!

RICO: Muchas gracias.

JED: Ole! Más presentos here. Coca Cola for the little lady. And for the Señora un credit carto!

VICTORIA: ¿Para qué se usa esto?

RAMONA: What function does this serve, Señor? I will translate for my parents until they learn your language.

JED: Which should be about any minute now. Tello your padre we hablar negocio later on. You folks just go right ahead with your fiesta, pretend I'm not here. . . .

RICO: Señor, ¿cuál es su misión aquí en California?

RAMONA: My father would like to know what is your mission here in California?

JED: Oh, sell a few beads, do some sightseeing. . . .

RICO: Pregúntale ¿por qué no le ha fregado a su negro?

RAMONA: Why haven't you beaten your slave? (Jed and Rufus look confused.) We hear tell that you Yankees delight in mistreating your slaves.

JED: What, me beat my nigger?! Why, el como mi sono. Aren't you boy?

RUFUS: (Aside.) We probably is related along de way.

RICO: (Trying to speak English.) You querer comer! (Makes eating motion.)

RAMONA: Would you like something to eat?

RICO: Salt carne? Corn pan?

JED: No, gracias, pero I could go for a burrito or a cold margarita! Ain't you got no Taco Bells 'round here?

RICO: Tonta, prepárale una comida al señor. My Tonta, she fixe you upe. Cuánto tiempar you estar aquí?

RAMONA: My father would like to know how long you plan to stay here in California?

JED: (*Looking at this wrist watch.*) What year is this? 1842? Oh, a couple of centuries, at least.

RICO: Señor, one cosa . . . muy important.

JED: Sir, I think you ready to speako el English.

RICO: Y you, señor, the Español.

JED: Claro, you hablo Español perfecto. Six weeks Berlitzo.

RICO: Ife you stay aquí por mucho tiempo . . . you deber ser ciudadano México . . . comprende? Very importante.

JED: Okay, okay. Let me tako uno siesto to thinko. After all, is this not the land of mañana?

RICO: Okay. I show you tu roomo. Tonta, el granero para el negro! (*Exit Tonta and Rufus.*) My Tonta show you slave barn.

JED: Wait a minuto. You folks no have to terminar fandango so earlyo! I heard you danco until dawno!

RICO: Is all right. Party over! (*Exit Rico and Jed in fervent discourse.*)

RAMONA: Buenas noches, Mamacita.

VICTORIA: ¡Qué Mamacita ni qué mi abuela! I know Joaquín was here! Drive him out of your mind, Ramona, he's gone forever! (*Ramona stalks out. Enter Rico.*) What's the matter, querido, you seem preoccupied?

RICO: It was something the Yankee said. He asked me why there were so few white people like us in the territory. And I could not help but note a tone of derision in his voice.

VICTORIA: Are you sure it wasn't your imagination?

RICO: And then I asked him if he was from New England and he said, "no, I'm from Texas."

VICTORIA: Texas!

RICO: Yes, the same Tejas they stole in 1836. The same Tejas which is now a slave state. Dios mío, time is moving by so quickly. It seems as though we conquered California only yesterday.

VICTORIA: Sí, and Mexico the day before. (*They exit. On another part of the stage Tonta is seen leading Rufus to the door of the stable.*) I must tell you, the maid overhead Ramona and Joaquín talking and . . . (*Trailing off.*)

TONTA: This is the barn, this is where you sleep, Mr. Nigaro.

RUFUS: My name isn't "nigaro," it's Rufus.

TONTA: Isn't that what the white man called you, "nigaro?"

RUFUS: Yes, but don't you call me that. My real name is Rufus, Rufus Smith.

TONTA: Smith, isn't that the white man's name?

RUFUS: A slave doesn't really have a choice. Your last name is what your master's name is. I've been bought and sold three times. My last name was Jefferson, but I was born with the name Washington. Come to think of it, I may be related to the father of the United States. Say, I heard them calling you "Tonta." What kind of name is that, Indian name?

TONTA: No, it's a Spanish name.

RUFUS: Are you an Indian? What kind of Indian are you?

TONTA: I am a Kemyia.

RUFUS: Keem—aaa-yaaa?

TONTA: Kemyia. People who hunt by the cliffs in the morning.

RUFUS: How come you aren't hunting in the cliffs any more?

TONTA: The white man came.

RUFUS: Oh. What does Tonta mean?

TONTA: (*Ignoring the question.*) Long ago, when my people dwelt on this land, my grandfather, Chacupe-Chanush was the Chief. We lived in wickiups and gathered berries and netted fish from the sea.

RUFUS: That sounds very familiar. . . .

TONTA: But then the Holy Fathers came and converted us to Christianity. Are you a Catholic, or do you still believe in the mumbo jumbo?

RUFUS: No girl, I'm a Protestant.

TONTA: A Protestant! Oh, good night! (*Turning to leave and crossing herself.*)

RUFUS: Say, wait a minute, stay here and talk a bit, we have a lot in common.

TONTA: Oh no, you're a Protestant! And besides that, you're a slave. I'm a free woman!

RUFUS: Now, now, now. Don't you put on no fancy airs with me. I suppose you cook and clean for them Californios from morning until night because you love them so much. You slave just like I do!

TONTA: No! Slavery is no more. Don Rico, how do you say, "abolished" it.

RUFUS: There are different kinds of slavery. Maybe you don't call it the same thing, but it doesn't make it any better. Huh, just because they made a Negro like Don Rico the governor, don't mean nothing.

TONTA: Don Rico is not a Nigero. He is Spanish.

RUFUS: Girl, you are pulling my leg. Your Don Rico is blacker than my black fanny and you're telling me he's Spanish! Oh Lord, don't make me laugh! Besides, what do you care what he is, he still treats you like a dog!

TONTA: Very well, Mr. Rufus, have it your way. Perhaps you'll stay around California and become governor yourself some day.

RUFUS: Well, maybe I will. But first I'll start by becoming the Mayor of Los Angeles.

TONTA: But for the time being, Señor Alcalde, here you sleep . . . with the mules!

RUFUS: Dang blast it! Can't get no respect! (*Getting ready his bedroll.*) I'm not going to be sleeping in barns all my life, no Ma'am. Matter of fact, right after this trip, if I make Master Jed a whole pile of money, I'm going to be free. He promised! He promised.

TONTA: Don't believe a word they say, Rufus. I worked all my life for Don Rico, but I'm still just a dumb maid to him. You know what Tonta means? I'll tell you. Tonta means stupid. That's what they call us. Don't let them make a tonto out of you, Rufus! (*She exits.*)

JED: (*On another part of the stage, Ramona is seen standing on her balcony, dreaming of Joaquín. Jed approaches her.*) Buenas noches, Señorita.

RAMONA: Oh! Good night, Mr. Smith! (*Turning to leave.*)

JED: Please, don't go inside yet! I have been trying to orient myself geographically. Could you tell me the name of the mountains to the north there?

RAMONA: Las Montañas de San Bernardino.

JED: Saint Bernard. And what's the name of the valley down there?

RAMONA: El Valle de San Fernando.

JED: Saint Ferdinand. There was an unusual amount of smog today.

RAMONA: Esmog? What is esmog?

JED: Smog is what you get when General Motors, Firestone and the oil companies buy up the Electric Trolley Car system.

RAMONA: Oh. (*Not wishing to appear unworldly.*) We are very isolated from the rest of the world, Mr. Smith. We have no, uh, electric systems, yet. We do have the natural beauty of the terrain.

JED: Oh yes, I can't wait to go to Disneyland. Señorita, how far are the pyramids from here?

RAMONA: Oh, Señor, you are mistaken. We have no pyramids here in La Cuidad de La Reina de Los Angeles del Río Porciúncula.

JED: Is that the full name of this city? Is it not rather long? Why don't you just call it Los Angeles or L.A.?

RAMONA: El Lay? Sounds obscene! Los Angeles, the city of the Angels, sounds heavenly.

JED: The city of Angels . . . the Lost Angeles! My God! I see it all now!

RAMONA: What do you see?

JED: It's the City of the Lost Angels, smoldering, there in the dark, the poisoned fumes, embers burning, the maws of Hell!

RAMONA: Hell?

JED: There amidst the metallic skyscrapers, smoke! And over there, in the east side, fire!

RAMONA: I see nothing! No smoke, no fire!

JED: Jesus Christ! Can't you hear the noise, that awful droning, the machines whining, sirens howling . . . and men, the lost angels, battling each other like demi-gods!

RAMONA: Mr. Smith, are you ill? Shall I call for a physician?

JED: My mind! My mind! It's burning!

RAMONA: What shall I do? What shall I do?

JED: Water! Water! (Ramona dumps water from a flowerpot on Jed's head.) Thank you, I needed that.

RAMONA: Are you well?

JED: Yes, yes, just a momentary burst of apocalyptic prophecy. I'll be all right. I have fits, er, visions.

RAMONA: You certainly possess a fertile imagination.

JED: I'll be okay.

RAMONA: Tell me, Mr. Smith, what vision or future do you see for yourself here in our fair city?

JED: I want to see commercial possibilities, not scenes of destruction.

RAMONA: We have need of more capital.

JED: All I want is a little piece of land. Orange County. I'll develop, but modestly, in harmony with the environment. A few condo-miniums, 7-11's, Dunkin Donuts. . . .

RAMONA: We have a very liberal immigration policy, there being but 6,000 of us Californios, and so much land for the taking. My father, the governor, has given many land grants away quite recently.

JED: Your father, what does he think of us Yankees?

RAMONA: He likes Mexicanized Yankees the best. Many of your people have come here and adopted our ways.

JED: I'll get me a sombrero and sarape. . . .

RAMONA: It takes more than that to become a Californio.

JED: I'll drink tequila, listen to mariachis. Say, what does your father think about California uniting with the United States?

RAMONA: God forbid! Don't let him hear you say that. He's a staunch Mexicano all the way. But I know that someday California will be free to decide her own destiny.

JED: You need help, you need someone to stand by your side.

RAMONA: We can handle our own affairs.

JED: No you can't! There's too many wolves and bears around. Look at the Ruskies, why they're already in Alaska. Next thing you know they'll be in El Salvador. You need the old Red and White and Blue beside you.

RAMONA: What can your country offer us?

JED: Uncle Sam can give you security and prosperity. Unite with us and you'll have apple pie and rock 'n roll, Mickey Mouse and the L.A.P.D.

RAMONA: We have no need of these things. We have our land and livestock, our stately churches and our merry fandangos, all of this here in Rancho Madera Acebo.

JED: Rancho Mad Era Azebo? What does that mean?

RAMONA: Literally, in English, the Ranch of the Wood Holly.

JED: Wood Holly? Woody Holly? Holly Woody. Hollywood! Hollywood! I see it all now!

RAMONA: Are you having another momentary apocalyptic fit?

JED: Hollywood and Vine! Groman's Chinese Theatre. The Brown Derby! Motion pictures! Panavision!

RAMONA: Should I get more water? Your eyes, they look like shooting stars!

JED: Stars! Stars! Movie stars! I'll make movies.

RAMONA: Un momento, por favor, slow down.

JED: (Climbing up on her balcony.) Let me explain. (Pulling out a photograph.) See this photograph of my mother, someday we'll be able to run thousands of these together into moving pictures. We'll project them on a screen and be able to control millions of people's minds!

RAMONA: This is your mother? Where was this photograph taken?

JED: In Europe, her name was Goldie, she's dead now. I'm her only son, promised I would carry her picture around with me forever, but that's another story.

RAMONA: What are you going to do with this invention?

JED: Make money! Become rich and powerful, I'll make porno movies. Open up a string of porno shops. Ninety-nine percent of the world's smut will come from El Lay. We'll do snuff films! After all, life is cheap in Latin America. No, just kidding! *(Down on his knees.)* Ramona, marry me! Don't you see, it's in the stars!

RAMONA: Señor, please, this sort of thing is not done here. Get off your knees!

JED: You'll marry me. You will marry me.

RAMONA: No, impossible! Besides, I am promised to someone else.

JED: Who? What's his name?

RAMONA: Joaquín! And he will kill you!

JED: Is that like Joaquin Valley?

RAMONA: Get off my balcony!

JED: All right, don't get mad. But how about a goodnight kiss? In our country it's perfectly proper to kiss a girl on the first date. Some couples even go further. Have you ever heard of Women's Liberation?

RAMONA: Did you say emasculation? No thanks.

JED: Well then, how about a stage kiss? It's only make believe!

RAMONA: *(Pushing him over the side of the balcony.)* Mañana to you, gringo! *(Ramona exits.)*

JED: No, don't say mañana! It's today. Eureka! I found it! Eureka!

RICO: *(Seen at another part of the stage writing at a desk.)* To the Honorable President of the Republic of Mexico. I am writing to you with a heavy heart. . . .

JED: *(Appearing at another writing desk.)* The conquest of California would be absolutely nothing. It would fall like a ripened fruit from its bough into the hands of the Anglo-Saxon race as the people here are incapable of defending it. *(Jed pulls out a pistol and slams it on the desk.)*

RICO: The uncertainty in which we find ourselves in this territory because of the excessive introduction of armed adventurers from the United States of the North leaves us no doubt of the war we shall have with them. *(Pulls out his own pistol and loads it.)*

JED: *(Addressing himself to the audience.)* Therefore, I say, let us strike now and free this blessed country from Mexican tyranny.

RICO: *(To the audience as well.)* The Departmental Treasury is exhausted. We have no standing garrison other than volunteers. Please, send money, men, and material at once. God and Liberty, Río Rico, Los Angeles, California. May 25, 1846.

JED: We'll take the capital, Monterey, and then by ship secure San Diego Bay.

RICO: *(To Jed.)* By what right do you have to do this?

69

JED: Manifest Destiny!

RICO: Thievery!

JED: You stole it from the Indians.

RICO: You shall not have it! Do you intend to persue your insidious goal of establishing slavery in California like you did in Texas?

JED: No! California will be free! Rufus! Rufus! *(Rico and Jed are face to face.)*

RUFUS: *(Running in with a rifle, followed by Tonta.)* Here I is!

JED: Cover my back, boy. Make sure it's a fair fight. You stick with me and you're free, hear?

RUFUS: I hear you.

JED: August, 1846. *(To the audience.)* We've met little resistence.

RICO: Mexicanos! Mexicanos! Do not fail your country now! Death to the invaders! *(Victoria and Ramona enter.)*

VICTORIA: ¡Rico, estamos contigo!

RICO: Ramona, send word to Joaquín. Tell him to come quickly!

RAMONA: Papá, will you let him marry me!

RICO: Of course! He's one of us. He's a Californio. *(Ramona kisses her father, then goes to whisper a message in Tonta's ear. Exit Tonta.)*

JED: Very well, shall we commence?

RICO: After you. *(The two combatants stand back to back, pistols in hand. There is a very dreamlike quality to this scene, performed to a slow minuet.)*

JED: *(As they pace away from each other.)* Quite obviously, my dear sir, you are incapable of governing this territory.

RICO: Excuse me, but what do you know of civilization? We founded universities in Mexico City before you landed your motley crew on the Mayflower.

JED: Yes, my dear sir, but we wrote the book on Democracy. You merely copied us, and a cheap imitation at that.

RICO: You deceived us in Texas. We welcomed you as equals and you stabbed us in the back.

JED: Remember the Alamo!

RICO: Racist!

JED: Half breed!

RICO: Gringo!

JED: Greaser! You're done fur. General Kearny, who just took all of New Mexico without a fight, is on his way to San Diego.

RICO: Wrong! Kearny was stopped at San Pasqual by my brother's California Lancers, the best horsemen in the world. Kearny's powder was wet and twenty of your men were cut down like steers. The rest are besieged and are forced to eat their mules!

JED: No! Everyone knows greasers are afraid to fight!

RICO: (*Shooting him down.*) What do you think of Mexican coward-ice now? Get back from whence you came, Yanqui!

JED: Not so fast. You may have won the battle . . . but look, look! All around you!

RICO: I see nothing. (*William Tell Overture.*) What's that?

JED: Listen! Listen! (*Confusion on the Mexican side as jets roar over-head.*) Up there, in the sky, it's a bird, it'a a . . . Stealth Bomber! (*Jets shake the set.*) It's the United States Air Force!

RICO: Air Force?

JED: Oh, you primitives! If only you knew the glory that awaits us! (*Bombs drop. Everyone but Jed runs for cover.*) Surrender! Surren-der! Or face total annihilation! If you stand in the way of prog-ress, we'll drop the atom bomb, so help us God! (*Aside.*) After all, they'se only colored people!

RICO: (*Dazed and confused, Rico hands over his pistol.*) ¡Mi pistola!

JED: At last! She's mine, all mine! California! (*While Victoria consoles Rico, Jed grabs Ramona.*) California!

RAMONA: No, no, no! Let me go! Let me go!

RICO: You can't have my daughter!

JED: I do believe I've taken her already! (*Handing him a document.*) Sign, sir, sign the surrender at Cahuenga Pass, January, 1847. (*Afterwhich he carries Ramona away kicking and screaming.*) Cali-fornia here I come! Right back where I started from! (*He exits.*)

RAMONA: My name is not California! It's Ramona! (*Exits.*)

RICO: ¡Dios mío, qué desgracia!

JOAQUIN: (*Rushing in.*) Don Rico, Doña Victoria, the Gringos . . .

RICO: We know. We lost the war.

JOAQUIN: Where is Ramona?

VICTORIA: The Gringo took her!

JOAQUIN: Oh my God! Which way? (*They point, he exits.*)

Act II

Place: *Rancho Hollywood. Meanwhile, back at the rancho, the Californios are lamenting their fate.*

RICO: I lost my daughter, I lost my state, what next?

JOAQUIN: We lost more than that, Don Rico, we lost the myth!

RICO: What myth are you talking about?

JOAQUIN: The myth of invincibility. Don't you see, the Gringos have out-conquered the conquistadores. The difference is that when the Spaniards came to Mexico they brought a statue of La Virgin de Guadalupe. The Gringos came to California and installed the dollar!

RICO: My son, what are you talking about? Have you gone crazy?

JOAQUIN: Crazy like a fox. That gives me an idea. Next time you see me I won't be dressed in sheep's clothing. Hasta la vista. *(He exits.)*

RICO: Strange boy! Still, I should have let him marry Ramona. Oh, Victoria, what a terrible state of affairs! And I thought we could retire in a grand style and truly enjoy our old age.

VICTORIA: Don't be so despondent, we can still work, we have our health. See this mountain stream, let's look for gold.

RICO: There is no gold, it's just a myth, like the story of Calafia, the Amazon Queen . . . our ancestors imagined it.

VICTORIA: Something glitters. *(She picks up a nugget.)* Look, I found a nugget!

RICO: It's probably fool's gold.

VICTORIA: No, bite into it, it's real! The rains have washed it down from the mountains.

RICO: *(Rico bites it.)* You're right! Gold! We better hurry, the Gold Rush is going to start any day. *(They start to pan.)*

JED: *(Entering with Ramona, dressed as gold miners. She wears a blonde wig.)* The miners came in Forty-Nine. . . .

RAMONA: The whores in Fifty-One. . . .

JED: And when they got together . . .

RAMONA: *(Pointing to Jed.)* They produced the native son!

JED: *(Pulling out a gun.)* All right! All right! The Miner Forty-Niner and his Darlin' Clementine run the claim jumpers off their stake!

RICO: *(Not recognizing them.)* I beg your pardon, Señor, but we found it first.

JED: I don't care, you are a foreigner. Only Natives can mine here.

RICO: I beg your pardon, Señor, my family has been here for over three generations.

JED: Clementine, what's he look like to you?

RAMONA: Faintly familiar. . . .

JED: Well, he looks like a damn greaser to me! (*Cocking his gun.*) Now, for the last time, if you want to mine here you have to pay a Foreign Miner's Tax.

RICO: But I told you, I am a Native Californio. (*Jed points the gun at him.*)

JED: You still look like a greaser from Sonora or Chile to me.

RICO: Señor, I want no trouble. I will pay the tax.

JED: That'll be $300 per month.

RAMONA: $300 dollars! But we won't be able to make a profit!

JED: Exactly.

RICO: This is our claim! We won't leave without a fight!

JED: (*Shooting at him.*) That's okay with me, greaser!

RAMONA: (*As Rico shoots back.*) Help, help, help! It's an insurrection!

JED: Don't give it any legitimacy! Your line is "help, the bandidos are robbing us!"

RAMONA: Oh yes, "kill the Frito Bandido!"

RICO: I am not a bandido. But you are turning me into a revolucionario!

JED: Kill the terrorists!

RICO: ¡Viva Villa!

RAMONA: Wait, Jed, I know that man. . . .

JED: Don't worry, we've got 'em surrounded. We'll starve them out!

RICO: I have run out of ammunition! Estamos perdidos.

VICTORIA: Is there no one who can save us from this fate?

RAMONA: No, don't shoot! He's my . . . (*Just as Jed is about to shoot Rico we hear the strains of "Zacatecas."*)

VICTORIA: Could it be? (*Enter Joaquín dressed like Zorro.*)

JED: Who is that?

RICO: El Zorro!

RAMONA: The fox!

JOAQUIN: No, it is I, El Zorrillo!

JED: El Zorrillo? What's that mean?

RAMONA: Run! Run for your life! (*Running in the direction of her parents.*) El Zorrillo means . . .

JOAQUIN: (*Throwing a skunk at Jed.*) Take that . . . you stinking Gringo!

RAMONA: Skunk!

JOAQUIN: (As he exits through the audience.) ¡El Zorrillo! ¡El Zorrillo!

JED: Oh my God!

RICO: Who was that masked man? He saved our lives!

(Up in the hills, Marcus, the soldier, has Gerónima, the Indian trapped in a cave.)

MARCUS: You gonna have to come down sooner or later, injun.

GERONIMA: Come up and get me, white man.

MARCUS: If you give up, I promise that no harm will come to you.

GERONIMA: You will shoot me.

MARCUS: No! We're supposed to take you to a reservation in Oklahoma.

GERONIMA: Huh, so you can give me a blanket full of smallpox and tuberculosis? No thanks, I stay here among the cactus.

MARCUS: Where you hear them crazy stories, injun?

GERONIMA: From my people.

MARCUS: I can't believe that! That is sick.

GERONIMA: It is also sick the way you slaughter buffalo from passing trains, white man.

MARCUS: I'm not a white man, I am black.

GERONIMA: You a black? I knew a black.

MARCUS: Born in New England. My Daddy's name was Washington. . . .

GERONIMA: I know you! Let me see your face! (As Marcus exposes himself Geronima fires a shot.)

MARCUS: God damn, crazy injun? What the hell you trying to do?

GERONIMA: I don't like the uniform you are wearing.

MARCUS: What's the matter with you? I'm just doing my job, I got nothing against you.

GERONIMA: They why you try to kill me, nigger?

MARCUS: Watch your mouth, red man, or I'll make a wooden Indian out of you! Jesus!

GERONIMA: Black man, what is your name?

MARCUS: Marcus.

GERONIMA: My name is Gerónima. Let us not fight each other. Get back on your horse and leave these hills.

MARCUS: I don't know . . .

GERONIMA: Oh, I see. Did Kemosabe promise you forty acres of OUR LAND?

MARCUS: No, yes, I mean he did, but that ain't the reason . . .

GERONIMA: Is Kemosabe going to free you like Lincoln *again*?

MARCUS: You pretty damn smart, for an injun!

GERONIMA: What is that supposed to mean? Just because I am red and did not go to Booker T. Washington University, you think I am stupid?

MARCUS: All right, look. I'm going to put down one of my rifles and just walk out of here.

GERONIMA: Thank you, we will make good use of that rifle.

MARCUS: I hope some day we can talk under more pleasant circumstances. You know, there was a time once in the Florida Everglades when the Seminoles and some runaway slaves got together and whupped old Hickory's ass. . . .

GERONIMA: (During this time Gerónima has managed to come up and over to surprise Marcus.) Hold it, soldier!

MARCUS: Oh Lordy!

GERONIMA: (Cocking her pistol.) One move and you go to the sacred grounds.

MARCUS: Look, I had you cornered, but I let you go. I gave you a rifle!

GERONIMA: I want to see how black you really are. Take off that uniform. Go on, strip! Black or white, soldier, you killed many of my people.

MARCUS: (Taking off his clothes.) I had no choice, I had no job, it was the only thing I could do! (Marcus throws his clothes in Gerónima's face and attacks her. They wrestle to the ground with Marcus on top.)

GERONIMA: Rufus!

MARCUS: Tonta! It's you! I almost killed you. What are you doing out here?

GERONIMA: I ran away to join the free tribes. Rufus, they're killing all of my people, just like the buffalo.

MARCUS: God, I'm so sorry! Did I hurt you? I'm so glad I found you again. Gerónima, I like that much better than Tonta.

GERONIMA: What are you going to do now, Marcus? Take me back to the white man? (Fade or blackout. Meanwhile, Ramona is trying to smooth things over between Jed and her parents.)

RAMONA: Mami, Papi, I'm so glad to see you!

VICTORIA: Ramona, ¿qué estás haciendo con ese blonde wig?

RAMONA: It's the new me, Mamá. Oh, Jed, honey, come and say hello to my parents.

RICO: He almost killed us!

RAMONA: Jed's not such a bad guy once you get to know him, Papá, you'll see. Jed, honey, come here!

75

JED: Good seeing you folks again. (*Aside.*) He looks like a nigra!

RAMONA: (*Holding her nose.*) Oh . . . not too close . . . down wind!

JED: My apologies for this unfortunate incident. From now on let us handle matters according to the letter of the law. The war is over. Why don't we sign the Treaty of Guadalupe Hidalgo? (*Handing Rico a document to sign.*)

RICO: Do you promise to honor the rights of all Mexicans in the new territories? Will you allow us the same rights accorded to the North Americans?

JED: Of course! (*Rico signs.*) Now, let's apply for statehood together. Hold up your right hand. (*Everybody does so.*) No, not yet, ladies! Do you swear to uphold the Constitution of the United States, so help you God?

RICO: Sí, I mean, yes.

JED: Congratulations. You are now an American citizen. (*Shaking his hand.*) Now, sir, would you do the honor of marrying me to your lovely daughter?

RICO: I am afraid you have already taken her.

JED: Let's make it legitimate. For future generations.

RAMONA: You see, Mamá, he's not so bad!

VICTORIA: ¡Ay, mi hija! (*Sniffling.*)

RICO: (*Acting as priest.*) Do you?

JED and RAMONA: We do!

RICO: (*Making the sign of the cross.*) You are! You may kiss the bride! Now, if you will excuse us, my wife and I must tend to our affairs.

JED: Not so fast, there's more documents to sign. (*Handing Rico a paper.*)

RICO: (*Signing it.*) What does it say? I can't read English.

JED: (*Whisking it away.*) You better learn. This is the Law of 1851, under which the burden of proof is placed on the land owner to defend the title to his land.

VICTORIA: (*Trying in vain to retract the paper.*) That means much time and money in court defending the rights to our land! That's not fair! What can we do?

JED: Write your congressman.

RICO: Who is he?

JED: Me.

RICO: We need someone in office who will understand the Mexicano.

RAMONA: Why don't you run, Papá? (*As Jed tries to shut her up.*)

RICO: Great idea! My people will vote for me. What do I have to do?

JED: Just sign this voter registration blank.

VICTORIA: Don't sign anything without reading it first.

RICO: Don't you have any forms in Spanish?

JED: Y'all in 'Merica now, ya gotta spick good English.

RICO: Ramona, ayúdame a leer esto.

RAMONA: Sí, Papá, just sign right here. There. He's registered now, right?

JED: Right, but only if he owns property.

RICO: But you just stole my lands!

JED: Sorry, that's showbiz! *(Whisking away the old rancho sign.)*

RICO: My rancho, what have you done to my rancho?

JED: *(Putting up the new sign.)* Don't worry, Don Rico, Rancho Hollywood will stay in the family!

ALL: Rancho Hollywood?

JED: Yes, clever name for a housing tract or apartment complex, don't you think? . . . which it will be eventually?

RICO: *(Going for Jed's throat.)* I'll kill you for this!

JED: Ah, ah, ah! I'll call the Highway Patrol! *(Enter Marcus.)* Rufus, just in time. Don Rico has a problem here abiding by our laws. *(Placing Marcus between himself and Rico.)*

RICO: *(Being restrained by Ramona, Victoria.)* He stole my lands, my rancho!

MARCUS: Just like you stole it from the Indians.

JED: Excellent, Rufus, you are learning so well.

MARCUS: The name isn't Rufus anymore, it's Marcus.

JED: My goodness, are we moving through time that fast? *(Handing Marcus a camera.)* Would you mind taking a photograph of Ramona and me kissing in front of our rancho? Fiery, impetuous Señorita and handsome Yankee soldier. Heal those old war wounds sort of thing. *(Aside to Marcus.)* Did you take care of our Indian problem?

MARCUS: I sure did . . . I married her! *(Enter Gerónima.)*

JED: What!

RAMONA: Tonta!

GERONIMA: The name is Gerónima.

JED: *(Taking Marcus aside.)* You married a squaw, just when we were nearing the final solution! I'll have your stripes for this. . . .

VICTORIA: Tonta, you're welcome to come live with us if you want.

GERONIMA: So I can be your maid? No thanks. From now on you be the maid!

JED: I'll bust you back down to buck private, you black buck you!

MARCUS: Now, you watch your mouth *Massa* Jed. I am a free man and a land owner. And me and this Kemyia woman are going way back in the hills where we can't be bothered by no white trash and raise us a whole lot of black and red children.

JED: You'll never make it alone, my boy, you'll need capital, letters of credit. Stay here, work for me.

MARCUS: I don't need a damn thing from you. All you ever done is cheat me from the day I was born.

JED: That's not true, I helped you out, I guided your way. I need you, Rufus, to help me build this country.

MARCUS: Get your Spanish boy there to do it. He'll probably work for less. (Marcus starts to exit with Gerónima.)

JED: Rufus! Rufus, don't go! We've been through so much together. Rufus, God damn it, I'm your Daddy!

MARCUS: (Returning.) What did you say?

JED: I said, I'm your father, boy. Your real father. Your Mama was a cook in the big house. She died when you were a baby. I took you with me on the sailing ship.

MARCUS: You've never been my father . . . and you never will! If I ever see you around me or mine again, I'll kill you! Do you hear me, motherfucker! (He exits.)

JED: How sharper than a serpents tooth!

RAMONA: Are you all right, Jed?

JED: Well, no use crying over spilled milk. He'll be back. They both will. Now then, let's get on with the business at hand. It's the dawn of the Twentieth Century, time to usher in a new era of peace and prosperity.

RAMONA: Do you really mean it? No more war, no more killing?

JED: Oh, maybe just a little charge up San Juan Hill. . . .

RICO: The Twentieth Century already? Why, it seems as though we just settled California yesterday.

VICTORIA: And Mexico the day before.

JED: Come, come, you already said those lines. We're going to have to find you some new ones.

RAMONA: Jed's right, Mamá, we Mexican-hyphen-Americans can't be living in the past.

RICO: Mexican-hyphen-Americans now, are we?

RAMONA: Papá, I've become a child of both cultures. And my name is not Ramona anymore, it's Ronny.

RICO: Roni? Ay, Ramona, ¡cómo te has perdido!

VICTORIA: Everything is changing so fast! I wish we could go back to the old days, life was much simpler.

RICO: There was order, family, tradition.

VICTORIA: Yes, and the fiestas and ferias. . . .

JED: Wait minute! I just thought of something!

RAMONA: Jed, are you having another vision!

JED: Yes! I see how we can use the past to find our future. Why don't we have an Old Spanish Days Fiesta and celebrate your Spanish heritage!

RAMONA: Mamá, doesn't that sound like a grand idea! *(Victoria is not convinced.)*

JED: See those old run down adobes and missions? We'll restore them, by golly. Start a Native Sons of the Golden West club. Dress up like Spaniards and ride through downtown Santa Barbara. Name a baseball team the "Padres." Don Rico can be the Grand Marshall.

RAMONA: You can wear your charro suit, Papá.

JED: Doña Vicky can ride side saddle in her mantilla.

VICTORIA: Ramona, help me fix my hair. *(Ramona does so.)*

RICO: I could do a few rope tricks with my lasso. You know that many things western, like rodeos and the lasso, came from the Mexican. We were the original vaqueros, what you call "buckaroos."

JED: Exactly, we'll have sangria, flamenco dancers, Taco Bells! Olé! Olé! We'll haul in tourists by the busloads. Real estate values will soar! We'll even make a movie out of it!

RAMONA: Ye Olde California Days, take two!

JED: No, we'll call it . . . RANCHO HOLLYWOOD! Ronny, I am going to make a star out of you! *(As the Ricos get ready for the next scene.)* But where can I find an extra hand? *(Jed has his camera in hand.)*

JOAQUIN: *(Entering, dressed like Cantinflas.)* Didi somee bodee callee for me?

JED: Ah, hah! A wetback!

JOAQUIN: No, a wet butt. *(Pointing towards his rear end.)*

JED: What's you name, boy?

JOAQUIN: Manual, Manual Labor.

JED: Perfect! You're just what I needed. You don't have any papers, do you?

JOAQUIN: No, Señor, that's how I got the wet butt. Me dio diarrea.

JED: Moctezuma's revenge, eh boy?

JOAQUIN: No, Sir, Gringo's revancha!

JED: What?

JOAQUIN: Too many Big Macs.

JED: Okay. Let's get to work.

JOAQUIN: ¡Orale, el jale!

JED: If everyone's ready, let's shoot the balcony scene. *(Jed assumes his old role as Director, Joaquín becomes the Cameraman.)*

JOAQUIN: Shut up, shut up! Get ready, get set!

VICTORIA: Wait a minute, isn't this the part we came in on?

RICO: Yes, we've been through this before. Who's going to play the male lead?

JED: *(Taking Rico's sombrero off his head.)* I am!

RICO: But . . . you're Anglo.

JED: No problem, I'll wear brown contact lenses!

RICO: But you are white, we Californios were . . .

JED: Spanish. I can pass . . .

RICO: No, no, no! We were everything, white, black, brown . . .

RAMONA: Black!

RICO: Yes, that's what we've been trying to tell him all along. But he insists upon saying we're Spanish!

JOAQUIN: *(To Jed.)* They are Mexican. Look how they have the nopal on their foreheads!

JED: I don't care! I've had it! Do it my way or get off the lot, now! *(To Joaquín.)* Film this! Film this!

RAMONA: Jed, honey, just give me a couple of minutes. Papá! You're ruining my scene! And what's all this about being black?

RICO: It's true, mi hija, I am a mulatto. My grandmother was black. Which means, you have some black blood also.

RAMONA: Me! Blonde Ronny Rico, star of the stage, screen and the Great White Way, black?

RICO: Ramona, it's nothing to be ashamed of.

VICTORIA: Your father didn't tell you sooner, dear, because we wanted to protect you.

RAMONA: If he finds out, this could be the end of my career!

JED: Well, what's it going to be?

RICO: Do I get a role?

JED: Yes, a non-speaking role!

RICO: That did it! You'll hear from my agent. ¡Vámonos, Victoria!

RAMONA: But Papá, where will you go, what will you do?

RICO: No importa, whatever is necessary. I'll go back to being a ranchero.

JED: That's ranch hand, Rico, I mean, "pobre." I own the land.

RICO: I don't care, at least it's honest work.

VICTORIA: Adiós, mi hija.

RAMONA: Goodbye, Mamá. Goodbye, Papá. *(She hugs her parents. They exit.)* My parents, they're gone!

JED: Let them go, Ronny, let them go and pick their . . . grapes of wrath. Huh, and I could have gotten them a Coors Distributorship in Montebello. Here, take some of this, it'll make you feel better. *(Offering her a vial of white powder. To Joaquín.)* Don't film this.

RAMONA: What is it?

JED: Cocaine. *(She declines. He shrugs his shoulders and snorts the entire vial.)* Dynamite!

RAMONA: You don't understand how much my family means to me. You don't care.

JED: Ronny, blow them off! I'm your father now, and that camera is your mother. *(Motioning to Joaquín to film.)* Yes, the audiences out there in the dark air-conditioned cinemas of America are your children.

RAMONA: What part am I playing . . . who am I?

JOAQUIN: *(Reading from the script.)* It says here that you are "the fiery, impetuous Ramona Rico."

JED: Forget that! You're Ronny Rocket, Latin spitfire, the hottest thing to hit Hollywood since Carmen Miranda.

RAMONA: *(Dancing and singing.)* Mamá no quiero, Mama no quiero . . . Maaaaa maaaaaa no quiero, no quiero . . .

JED: Get a close up of these beautiful Spanish tits! You've heard of "Spanish Eyes," well . . .

JOAQUIN: ¡Ahora, sí, que se está pasando!

RAMONA: Jed, what are you trying to do?

JED: Ronny, I've fallen behind schedule. The backers are breathing down my neck. I have to hit paydirt. We're going to do a sex scene sooooooo torrid it'll have them panting in their Guccis.

RAMONA: What kind of sex scene?

JED: One with rising and falling action, one that reaches a climax in technicolor and panavision.

RAMONA: What's my line? Line!

JOAQUIN: ¡Chinga tu madre, güey!

RAMONA: Chinga tu maaaa . . . Jed, we can't do that on the screen!

JED: Why not? We're married.

RAMONA: You forget, we divorced last year, remember, after you had that affair with the football player?

JED: Ronny, you're too much of a conformist.

RAMONA: Jed, I thought you wanted to do art, not smut!

JED: Forget about that. Think about the Mercedes 450 SL with your own private license plate, the million dollar mansion in Beverly Hills, your name, Ronny Rocket, cast in diamonds on the marque.

RAMONA: My name is Ramona Rico.

JED: Okay. Whatever! Now, are we going to do the scene or not?

RAMONA: I don't know, my heart isn't in it.

JED: All right, my little chile pepper, have it your way. I'll just get a Gringa to do your part.

RAMONA: Jed, how could you, after all we've been through to-gether!

JED: There are thousands of players in this town who would just die for a part in a Jedediah Goldbanger Smith Production. I'll just put a casting call up on the board. (*Turning to leave.*) Stick around, Chico, I'll be right back.

RAMONA: A Gringa, he's going to get a Gringa.

JOAQUIN: Sabes qué, ever since the talkies there have been Gringo actors in this town making their living playing Latino roles. And you know something else, there were some Latino actors like Roland Navarro who could only play white roles because they were not dark enough!

RAMONA: (*Taking off her blonde wig.*) It gets rather confusing, doesn't it? No wonder I'm so screwed up. Say, don't I know you from somewhere?

JOAQUIN: You may have seen one of my movies from Mexico. I am known as Tin Can, among other things. Oye, what are you going to do now?

RAMONA: I don't know. I could play it his way, get off the lot or shoot him to death.

JOAQUIN: There is another way, Ramona, we could form our own company like the original "United Artists." (*Jed enters before she can answer.*)

JED: Well, my little Taco Belle, have you decided what to do?

RAMONA: I'm going to stay here, this is where I belong.

JED: Ahhh, but it may be too late. Someone else may get the part. (*As Sinmuhow and Malcolm enter.*) Here they come for the audition. Rufus! Is that you? You old sonofabitch, I knew you'd return.

MALCOLM: (*Slapping his hand away.*) The name is Malcolm!

JED: Oh, right on, Malcolm. Got any experience?

MALCOLM: I have played many parts: slave, worker, soldier, invisi-ble man.

JED: Invisible man?

MALCOLM: People, especially white people, never look at me. They pretend I am not there or else they want to forget about me.

JED: Malcolm, we're doing a film about the Old California days. We're looking for a Mexican half-breed type. You could probably pass.

MALCOLM: They aren't much better off than we are.

JED: Try this bandana on, it'll cover your Afro.

MALCOLM: Is this like when white folks used to put on black face?

JED: It's a non speaking role, Kunta, do you want it?

MALCOLM: Ain't you got no part for a black revolutionary?

JED: No, not at the moment. Maybe later on we can work you into some kind of black action flick. You know, Shaft vs the marauding Mau Maus! Who's next?

SINMUHOW: I am Sinmuhow . . .

JED: How! A little Native American action. Come right on in, you don't even need a "reservation."

SINMUHOW: Sinmuhow, Spirit Woman, woman who knows many things.

JED: Sorry, we don't need anybody like that. That part calls for a silent sexy Latina to make it with the Spanish scion, me. Have you ever done any skin flicks?

SINMUHOW: No, but I have been a slave, maid, concubine . . .

JED: Don't worry, you could do this part lying down. Try on this zarape, very authentic.

SINMUHOW: But I am a real person, my spirit is real. I cannot play a wooden Indian.

JED: Well then, let's play cowboys and Indians!

SINMUHOW: Only if we play Custer's Last Stand.

JED: Very funny! Who's next? We're Equal Opportunity Employers.

JOAQUIN: I am. Don't you remember me? I'm one of the latest in your long line of stereotypes. I am your combination sleepy peon, Frito Bandido, Zorro, Cantinflesque, vato loco, wetback.

JED: Hey, how about a little gang exploitation film set in the smoldering East Los barrio, huh? No? Well then, Kunta, how about a Bojangles movie? Let me see you dance, I know you got rhythm. *(Jed dances, the rest of the players remain silent as they close in around him.)* Mr. Booooooo-jangles, dance, dance, dance. Sinmuhow! How about a nice wholesome maize commercial, huh? You know: "Our ancestors scalped settlers and at the end of the day were rewarded by the golden goodness of maize." *(Hop-*

ping around on one foot.) Whooop! Whooop! Whooop!

MALCOLM: I have a better idea, why don't we do a "kill whitey" film.

JED: No, no, that could be labled communist propaganda. Besides, who would pay to go see it?

RAMONA: The liberals.

JED: That's right, make them feel ashamed of being white.

RAMONA: Jed, don't you see, these distortions have twisted the minds of generations of children. Is this really how you see us?

JED: You too, huh. I always knew you were one of them.

RAMONA: That's right, I am. I am black and brown and white. And I'm proud of it.

JED: Oh yeah, well let me tell you something. I'm a minority too. I'm part Jewish, just like Barry Goldwater. My grandmother Goldie, remember? We've been persecuted for over 2000 years just because they say we killed Christ, Jesus!

JOAQUIN: Ladies and gentlemen, we are gathered here today to roast a great American filmmaker over the coals.

JED: Please, please! You're all taking this much too seriously. After all, it's only make believe!

JOAQUIN: We, the assembled representatives of all the so-called minorities, although we are actually in the majority now, want to pay homage to you, Jedediah Goldbanger Smith. . . .

JED: Wait a minute, aren't you missing someone? Where's Charlie Chan? Where's our slant eyed little nip? *(Assuming martial arts stance.)* Toyota! Datson! Sony! Mao! Chop Suey!

JOAQUIN: Jed, thank you, from the bottom of our hearts, for the creation of such memorable stereotypes, for the advancement of collective inferiority complexes, for the maligning and desecration of our cultures and for the loss, theft, and distortion of our history.

JED: Don't forget the wops and the micks and the polacks and the frogs and the . . .

JOAQUIN: We hereby present you with this mask as a token of our esteem. *(They ceremoniously hand Jed a redneck pig mask.)*

RAMONA: Jed, you really must change your image!

JED: My image? My image! Oh no, I couldn't accept this, really. I just want to thank all of those hardy pilgrims and pioneers for making all this possible. *(Strange nightmarish music. Lights low. Alone. Despite himself, he tries the mask on.)* I'm afraid this doesn't really fit me! Wait! Cut the scene! Cut the scene! Cut!

Cuuuuuuuuuuuutttt! (*Blackout. On another part of the stage, Rico and Victoria exit as though from a movie theatre, dressed in evening clothes.*)

VICTORIA: God, wasn't that a fantastic movie! *Variety* called "Rancho Hollywood the most profound statement ever made about the history of California."

RICO: I still can't believe that Joaquín, Malcolm, Jed, Ramona, all worked to make this project a success.

VICTORIA: Oh, and wasn't Ramona wonderful? I bet she gets nominated for an Oscar. Oh, how I wish we could have stayed on to work in the film.

RICO: Don't worry, I hear there might be a sequel. Well, there's the reception. Good thing we have our passes, otherwise we'd never get past security. Everybody who is anybody in Hollywood is here tonight.

VICTORIA: (*As they enter the central area, showing an imaginary guard their passes.*) Oh, there they are! Drinking champagne. (*We see the others partying.*)

RICO: Don't be obtrusive, let them enjoy the limelight.

SINMUHOW: The Executive Producer of Programming for CBS told me he wants to do a series based on Rancho Hollywood.

MALCOLM: Is that so? An agent for the Shuberts told me they want to stage it on Broadway.

JED: Hey, aren't you glad we buried the hatchet and got down firme! Hah! Ha!

JOAQUIN: Orale, especially since we are all equal partners in the production.

RAMONA: I was just told: Rancho Hollywood has seven Oscar nominations!

JED: Why not? It grossed twenty million in the first two weeks.

JOAQUIN: Let's drink to that! (*They all toast.*)

VICTORIA: (*To Rico.*) I can't believe this, I'm so proud of them.

RICO: Everything we worked for has come true.

SINMUHOW: (*To Malcolm.*) You know, all of a sudden I have all this money I don't know what to do with.

MALCOLM: I put my bread back into the ghetto. I bought a controlling interest in a chain of liquor stores.

SINMUHOW: I know what you mean. I went back to the reservation and started looking into prime investment properties.

RICO: Liquor stores? Buying land on the reservations?

JED: Well, Joaquín, how is the world of art these days?

RAMONA: Oh, he's been painting some beautiful murals a la Orozco, Rivera, Siqueiros.

JED: Public art?

JOAQUIN: Not exactly, man, those pinche homeboys keep spray-painting my murals.

JED: Like I always said, the masses don't really appreciate these things.

JOAQUIN: So now I do mostly interiors, you know, the Bank of America, Hilton Inn, places like that.

RICO: Victoria, this doesn't sound right. . . .

RAMONA: Well my broker is E. F. Hutton. And E. F. Hutton says . . . (*Everybody but Rico and Victoria Freeze.*)

RICO: Have they forgotten everything? Wake up! ¡Despierten! (*Speaking to deaf ears.*) Don't think only of your own greed and profit! You have a powerful tool at your disposal, use it!

VICTORIA: Rico, it's no use, they can't hear you.

RICO: All the social gains we made in the past . . . in danger of being swept aside. Listen to me, we, the elderly, the poor, they want to take away our social security, medicare, food stamps . . .

VICTORIA: Don't forget equal rights for women.

RICO: Affirmative action, everything! Don't turn your backs on us, please! Listen to us! Listen! (*They all come to.*)

JED: Attention! Attention, everybody! I have an announcement to make. First of all, I want to thank each and everyone of you for giving me another chance to prove to the entire world that Americans of different races, religions, and creeds can work together. That was very "white" of you! (*Everybody laughs.*)

ALL: All right! Let's here it! Orale, etc.

JED: My friends, you all know of my deep involvement with the Screen Actor's Guild, and although some have said I might make a fine governor of this golden state, I have decided to take on an even more difficult directorial responsibility because, I, for one, believe that this country has suffered long enough!

ALL: You can count on us! We're with you!

RICO: What in the devil is he talking about?

JED: Spread the word, tell everyone. We'll be needing script writers, P.R. people, make up artists, producers, everything that it takes to make a fantasy like Rancho Hollywood come true. My friends, I have decided to run for President of the United States of America! (*Silence. Everyone, except for Jed, looks at the audience. Slow fade.*)

Los Dorados

CHARACTERS

TUPIPE
CAPITAN
SARGENTO
PADRE
SINMUHOW
SIMQUALE

SINMUHOW: Damas y Caballeros, Ladies and Gentlemen, the play you are about to see, *Los Dorados*, is a mixture of fact and fiction about the clash between Native Americans and Spanish Conquistadors in Southern California. *Los Dorados* means the golden ones en español; golden, because all have come to these shores in search of what is precious . . . be it gold, converts, fame or simply work. *(Enter a native woman, Tupipe, who kneels before a campfire cooking. From the opposite side enter Capitán wandering aimlessly, lost and hungry. He reaches for a fruit from a tree and breaks the branch as she hears the sound and looks up. He tries to eat the fruit without peeling it and tosses it away with disgust as she rises and walks cautiously towards the sound. He crashes in the underbrush towards her as she draws her bow and arrow. He trips and falls and she draws back the arrow and is about to shoot. He sees her, rises, draws his sword and totters, nearly exhausted. She notes his sad condition and lowers her guard. He backs away from her and puts his sword down on the ground as she lays her bow and arrow on the ground. They walk tentatively towards each other. She picks a fruit from the same tree he did and peels it for him. He devours it ravenously. He pulls out some coins and gives one to her and she takes it, bites it, spits it out and returns it with disgust. He takes a small mirror out of his pocket and gives it to her and she stares at it in astonishment.)*

TUPIPE: Chacupe-Chanush?

CAPITAN: ¿Calafia? ¿Calafia de California?

TUPIPE: *(Gesturing around her.)* Kemyia. Kemyia. *(Pointing to herself.)* Tupipe Tunun. Kemyia!

CAPITAN: Soy Capitán Vizcaíno. Vengo de España, Europa. Vine en barco. *(He starts to mime a sailing ship.)* Del otro lado del mar.

TUPIPE: Del mar . . . *(Tupipe fades out as we enter Scene II. A boat at sea. Enter Laguna, LaJolla, etc.)*

SGT. LAGUNA: *(At the helm, singing to the tune of "Valencia.")*
    ¡Hortencia! No te sientes en la cama
    porque haces pestilencia!
    ¡Hortencia! ¡No te sientes en la cama
    porque haces pestilencia!
    ¡Pestilencia! ¡Pestilencia!

PADRE LAJOLLA: *(Kneeling and praying.)*
    ¡Padre Santísimo, ayúdanos a encontrar el Paraíso!
    ¡Padre Santísimo, ayúdanos a encontrar el Paraíso!

CAPITAN: *(Heaving over the side.)* Ayyyyyhayyyyyyyaaaaaaa!!!

PADRE: Sargento Laguna, what is the name of this ocean?

SGT: I don't know, Padre LaJolla, but we can call it anything you want.

PADRE: It's so serene and calm.

SGT: Yes, like the water in a newborn baby's bath. That's it, let's call it El Mar Del Agua de Baño! The Ocean of Bathwater.

PADRE: No, no, no! It's got to have more meaning. It must be prophetic. Feel how quiet, blue and at peace it is? Like the Virgin Mother herself. That's it! Let's call it El Mar de La Virgen Madre! The Ocean of the Virgin Mother!

SGT: Not that again!

PADRE: You never agree with anything I say!

CAPITAN: Are you two at it again? Haven't you figured out where we are?

PADRE: Mar de La Virgen Madre!

SGT: Ocean of Bathwater!

CAPITAN: *(Heaving.)* There's nothing pacific about this ocean!

PADRE: That's it, the pacific, El Pacífico!

SGT: Good compromise. The Pacific! *(They shake hands.)*

CAPITAN: Oh God, what I wouldn't do to get off this ship and back on dry land again!

SGT: Do you know what I like best about discovering new lands and people? You can name them anything you want. Indians, America, Fresno, Boca Ratón.

PADRE: No, those names are too common, hombre.

SGT: I'm a common hombre.

PADRE: We need names that will give our settlers divine inspiration, like San Diego, Santa Mónica, Sacramento, San Andreas.

SGT: I find fault with those names.

PADRE: But my names are blessed by Dios! And centuries from now, when people say Nuestra Señora La Reyna de Los Angeles an image of the Virgin will appear.

SGT: Not along Hollywood Boulevard it won't.

CAPITAN: For the last time! Does anybody know where we are?

SGT: By my reckoning, sir, we are somewhere to the right of the Indies.

PADRE: But in very close vicinity to Paradise!

CAPITAN: Have you all gone mad? No wonder we're lost! Oh God!

PADRE: Amen!

CAPITAN: What in the hell are we doing here? What are we looking for?

SGT: Spices, mi Capitán, spices!

CAPITAN: See what I mean! What do we need spices for, we haven't even got any food!

SGT: Plenty of rum left, sir. *(Capitán goes off to heave again.)*

PADRE: He's sick in a bad way.

SGT: I told him not to eat those chili peppers.

CAPITAN: Won't somebody please tell me where we're going? *(In between heaves.)* Oh, the devil take you all!

PADRE: Capitán, if you pardon my saying so, sir, you ain't got no faith.

CAPITAN: I knew I should have stayed in Spain. Anything but sea duty!

PADRE: Have faith! Have faith! Santa Fe! Wherever España goes, so goes the Holy Cross. La Santa Cruz! Santa Cruz, that's a good name.

SGT: And wherever España goes, so goes the big stick. *(Raising his club.)* El Palo Alto!

PADRE: Very good, Laguna!

CAPITAN: Fools! You think that alone will make the conquest! You need vision, vision, do you hear me?! Almighty vision! There, there in the horizon, I see a new and wonderful land!

PADRE: Land! Land! I don't see any land!

CAPITAN: I see a great and golden land run by a tribe of fierce and bloody Amazons! Women who wear trappings of solid gold, the only metal to be found there!

SGT: Gold, gold . . . did you say gold!

CAPITAN: Yes, and these Amazons are ruled by a queen, a tall and stately queen named Calafia. Calafia! She is black like a Moor. And her kingdom is called California . . . California!

ALL: California!

SGT: Steady as she goes, a sudden wind kicks up! The sails fill with air.

PADRE: A good sign, a righteous sign.

SGT: I must to the helm, we're starting to list.

CAPITAN: It's a gale! It's a storm!

SGT: The wind blows me back.

PADRE: The sky darkens, lightning and thunder!

SGT: Lash yourselves to the mast!

PADRE: *(Kneeling and praying.)* Padre Santísimo, vamos al Paraíso!

SGT: *(At the helm.)* Hortencia, no te sientes en la cama porque haces pestilencia!

CAPITAN: Calafia! Calafia! *(Sergeant and Padre exit, leaving Capitán alone. He looks around for the native woman.)* Calafia? Calafia? *(He exits and enter Tupipe and Sinmuhow very excited.)*

TUPIPE: I tell you, Sinmuhow, woman who knows many things, I saw a man, a man on the beach.

SINMUHOW: Tupipe, little sister, warrior to be, how can you be sure?

TUPIPE: It was just as you described it in your stories of times past. It had hair on its face, a voice like a frog, deep and hoarse, and no breasts!

SINMUHOW: Could it be, could it really be . . . Chacupe-Chanush?

TUPIPE: I asked if it was Chacupe-Chanush, your grandson, but it answered in a strange and foreign tongue.

SINMUHOW: Would that it were, Chacupe-Chanush, my grandson, returned from his voyage to the underworld.

TUPIPE: As was prophesied.

SINMUHOW: Lead me there, and quickly.

TUPIPE: Yes, blind mother, woman who sees many things.

SINMUHOW: Shhhhhhhhh! I hear someone coming!

TUPIPE: I don't hear anything.

SINMUHOW: My ears, they see, my eyes are deaf.

TUPIPE: It is my sister, Simquale-Simquala!

SINMUHOW: Hail Simquale, Chief of the Kemyia.

SIMQUALE: Hail Sinmuhow, woman who knows many things.

SINMUHOW: Your sister, Tupipe, warrior to be, informs me that she saw a man on the beach.

SIMQUALE: What? Is this possible. If true, we must slay it at once.

TUPIPE: But why would you do that, Chief sister? It meant no harm, it was hungry. I gave it fruit to eat.

SINMUHOW: Silence! Respect your elders, and the children who follow will do the same.

SIMQUALE: Tupipe, you know full well how they tried to enslave us many years ago. Therefore, all men must die!

SINMUHOW: All but one, my grandson, Chacupe-Chanush, he who will return from the underworld.

TUPIPE: Why him and not all the others?

SINMUHOW: Because he is pure of spirit and because he is to mate with the women from our tribe to propogate the species. Know full well, know now, that you are to be his first bride.

SIMQUALE: And know full well that I shall be his last bride, for after he has mated with me he will be sacrificed.

TUPIPE: No, that's terrible! How could you do that?

SINMUHOW: This child! I sometimes wonder if she has strength enough to be a Kemyia.

SIMQUALE: Tupipe! this is our way of life! Do not argue, or the youths who come after you will do the same.

SINMUHOW: Look at her, she cries!

TUPIPE: I am sorry.

SIMQUALE: Be courageous, as a lioness! *(Circling around her.)*

SINMUHOW: Be fierce, as a she-bear. *(Joining the circle.)*

SIMQUALE: Grow fangs, my she-bear.

SINMUHOW: Grow claws, my lioness.

SIMQUALE: Be as wily as a she-wolf.

SINMUHOW: With a sting like a black widow spider! *(All exit.)*

SGT: *(Entering from the opposite side, with Padre and Capitán.)* Shall I plant our standard upon this shore, sir?

CAPITAN: Yes, yes . . . hurry, before someone else does. The bloody British are everywhere.

PADRE: And let us also plant this cross here, to claim these lands in the name of Christ.

CAPITAN: Yes, yes, before the Moslems do.

PADRE: *(Kneeling.)* I pray to Almighty God that he consecrate our Holy Conquest.

CAPITAN: I hereby take possession of these lands in the name of the King of Spain, Carlos III, in this the year of Our Lord, 1542.

SGT: ¡Que viva España! ¡Que viva el Rey!

TUPIPE: *(Entering with Sinmuhow, Simquale from the other side of the stage.)* Look! There's the man I spoke of! There are others with him!

SIMQUALE: To arms! Stand ready to attack!

SINMUHOW: Wait! What are they doing?

TUPIPE: They are holding some form of ceremony on the beach.

SGT: *(As both groups move closer to the center.)* It's amazing, just look at this map. Since 1492 since old Columbus sailed the ocean blue . . . all that land we've discovered!

PADRE: Must have added at least one hundred leagues today. I wonder what the name of this place is? Look at that charming little cove to the south.

SGT: Padre LaJolla, it would please me very much if we named it after you, LaJolla Cove.

PADRE: Why, that's very nice of you. And look at that beautiful beach to the north. Why don't we call it Sgt. Laguna Beach!

SGT: I am honored . . . let's just write that down on the map.

CAPITAN: Wait! Stop! Look! There on the sand dunes! Amazons!

PADRE: Good God in heaven!

SIMQUALE: Now sisters, let your arrows fly!

TUPIPE: But what if it's Chacupe-Chanush!

SGT: Let's go back to the ship, let's go back to Spain, there's too many of them! *(Looking for someplace to hide.)*

PADRE: The Cross will protect us!

CAPITAN: Wait, wait, they mean no harm . . .

SGT: *(Slapping a mosquito on his neck.)* I've been shot by a dart!

CAPITAN: *(Drawing his sword.)* Stand fast! Remember that we are Spanish soldiers!

SIMQUALE: Charge into them!

SINMUHOW: *(Breaking in between the two groups just before they come to blows.)* Wait! By the eye of the sun, by the breath of the wind, wait! Speak to one another, speak! *(Drawing the Capitán to her, "reading" his face with her hands.)* My son, tell me, who are you?

CAPITAN: Capitán Cortez Cabrillo, en el servicio del Rey de España, a sus órdenes.

SIMQUALE: Cabrillo?

SINMUHOW: No, my son, speak English, so all those people *(Pointing to the audience.)* out there can understand you.

CAPITAN: *(With an American accent as a portent of things to come.)* Captain Cortez Cabrillo, in the service of the King of Spain, at your service.

SINMUHOW: Español . . . Spanish?

CAPITAN: I'm not Spanish, actually, I'm . . . Portuguese, Portugués!

SINMUHOW: Oh, all you Latinos look alike. Come, come with me, you are welcome, we shall hold a feast in your honor tomorrow night.

CAPITAN: Muchas gracias, and here is a small present for all of you. *(He hands out frisbees and Coca-Cola.)*

TUPIPE: Oh, Capitán, remember me!

CAPITAN: Why yes, the little Amazon I met on the beach. How are you dear! *(Moving on to Simquale.)* Excuse me, but aren't you Calafia, the Amazon Queen?

SIMQUALE: I am Simquale-Simquala, Chief of the Kemyia.

CAPITAN: Isn't this California?

SIMQUALE: No, this is the land of the Kemyia, people who hunt in the cliffs by morning.

CAPITAN: This isn't San Diego?

SIMQUALE: No, the names we give this land are Otay, Jamul,

Jamacha, Cuyamuc.

CAPITAN: We must have taken a wrong turn somewhere, those freeways are treacherous.

SGT: *(To Sinmuhow.)* Oh, golden mother, what beautiful bracelets you have. Are they of solid gold?

SINMUHOW: No, my son, they are made of what you call *fool's gold*.

PADRE: *(To Tupipe.)* Little girl, come here, don't be afraid. I have another present for you. *(Handing her a cross.)*

TUPIPE: What do I do with it?

PADRE: Wear it next to your breast, for it is a sacred cross.

SINMUHOW: *(Leading them to their abode.)* Now, this is your wickiup, here you rest, sun has fallen.

SGT: Wickiup? You mean tepee, don't you?

TUPIPE: She means wickiup!

SINMUHOW: Our wickiup is your wickiup.

CAPITAN: Nuestra casa es su casa . . . I like that saying! Thank you, I think I'm going to like this wickiup very much!

SINMUHOW: *(Noticing the cross around Tupipe's neck.)* Tupipe-Tunun, where did you get this? Give it back, right now. *(The Padre glares at Sinmuhow who takes her own symbol, a round "O" and puts it around Tupipe's neck.)*

CAPITAN: Señoras, excuse us, we have had a long journey and are very weary. Buenas noches, good night. *(Exit men.)*

TUPIPE: That Capitán is such a gentleman.

SINMUHOW: But he is not my son, Chacupe-Chanush!

SIMQUALE: Shall we kill them now?

SINMUHOW: More of their kind will be coming. Let us study them, for now. Keep a strong guard and we'll decide what to do with them tomorrow. *(All exit except for Tupipe.)*

TUPIPE: Night time is falling   *Dee nai-ma-y-ha-yo
  the day is ending May-yo ma-kwee-e toy yoi yoi
  clouds are coming Mata amama kay-ma ma-yo aye-yo
  winds are coming Ma kwee-e toy yoi yoi
  dance, dance
  clouds are coming.

(Tupipe falls asleep, is abruptly awakened in the morning by Simquale who has come to take her turn at sentry duty. The Capitán, meanwhile, has awakened. He does some exercises and washes his face in a

---

*Kemyia puberty rites.

nearby stream. Then he starts counting off rows in a checkerboard pattern as Simquale watches from the side.)

CAPITAN: Uno, dos, tres . . . cuatro, cinco, seis . . .

SIMQUALE: What are you doing?

CAPITAN: Nothing, just counting off the streets.

SIMQUALE: You mean these paths here, what for?

CAPITAN: For purposes of surveying. You know, land grants, housing tracts, condominiums!

SIMQUALE: Condominiums?

CAPITAN: Observe. We call this path here "A" Street and the one perpendicular to it, "First" Street. Then Second Street, Third Street and so on. The ones that cross one and two and three we can call B and C and D and so on. What do you think, Calafia?

SIMQUALE: The name is Simquale-Simquala! And I don't like those names at all. They show no imagination. This is the Path of the Rising Sun, for it runs to the high eastern hill . . . and the one that crosses it is the Way of the Morning Fog, for it runs to the ocean.

CAPITAN: Very poetic, I agree. But we have to simplify things for the masses. If this is to be the commercial center of San Diego someday, we have to make sure the postman can deliver the mail.

SIMQUALE: San Diego? I told you, this is the land of the Kemyia. By what authority are you doing this?

CAPITAN: The authority vested in me by the King of Spain. Observe, I even have a letter written by his Royal Majesty: *(Reading.)* "To Whom It May Concern, this is to introduce Capitán Cortez Cabrillo Vizcaíno . . ."

SIMQUALE: Vizcaíno? I thought you said your name was Cabrillo?

CAPITAN: It is Cabrillo, but it is also Vizcaíno. We have long names and just keep adding them on. *(Reading on.)* "Kindly tender Capitán Vizcaíno all due hospitality and facilitate his discovery of Alta or Upper California, as he is acting under the power vested in me as reigning sovereign of Spain, the Indies, the Philippines and Spanish Harlem." Signed, Felipe III, Rey de España, 1602.

SIMQUALE: 1602? Wait a minute! Why are we jumping dates so fast. It was just 1542 a few pages ago!

CAPITAN: Merely the dramatist's way of condensing history.

SIMQUALE: Just a minute, Cabrillo, Vizcaíno or whatever your name is. Just what are you planning to do here?

CAPITAN: Design, calculate, subdivide. Nothing more. Don't be afraid. I won't hurt anyone. This is just my red tape. (*Playing with red tape.*)

SIMQUALE: Capitán, you had better listen while I explain how we do things around here.

CAPITAN: Go ahead, I'm listening. (*As he continues with his red tape.*)

SIMQUALE: Our life is guided by our mother, the sun, and her daughter, the moon. The only charts we plot are those set by the stars. The air is our breath, the rain our blood. Our guiding spirit is the force of nature, and her direction is not made up of lines or angles, but rather of circles that re-occur again and again.

CAPITAN: We're going to have to find a way to control this stream.

SIMQUALE: Why not let it run its natural course?

CAPITAN: Plumbing, we'll invent plumbing! We'll take these long pipes, stick them into the stream, and run them into the wickiups and factories.

SIMQUALE: What for?

CAPITAN: To dispose of the waste that we, industry, will excrete. We'll invent toilets!

SIMQUALE: What are toilets?

CAPITAN: Toilets will be enamel or porcelain bowls that will flush one liter of waste with three liters of water.

SIMQUALE: There's one thing I don't understand. Where does the waste finally end up?

CAPITAN: Hell, who cares. In the bay, back in the water table.

SIMQUALE: Capitán, I do believe you are getting all wound up in your own contradictions. (*Capitán has slowly wound himself up in his red tape.*)

CAPITAN: We'll have parking lots, freeways, Taco Bells . . .

SIMQUALE: (*Helping him get unwound.*) You have such a fine imagination. If only you would come down to earth. Why don't I take you up to that lofty mountain where you can contemplate the world in solitude.

CAPITAN: Solitude. Yes, soledad. Soledad, great name for a correctional facility, make them think, make them suffer . . .

SIMQUALE: Correctional facility?

CAPITAN: Yes, a jail where troublemakers will be locked up.

SIMQUALE: But that just makes people worse.

CAPITAN: We gotta have justice in this colony.

SIMQUALE: (*As they exit together.*) Capitán, let me tell you a thing or two . . .

SINMUHOW: *(Entering with Tupipe.)* Where is your sister, Simquale?

TUPIPE: I saw her walking up the mountain with El Capitán.

SINMUHOW: Has all discipline broken down here? *(Hearing the other men stirring.)* Listen, the other men are stirring.

PADRE: Sargento Laguna, rise and shine! *(Coming out of the wickiup.)* Come on, hombre, there are souls to save, civilization to spread.

SGT: *(Popping his head out.)* We ain't even conquered this place yet.

PADRE: Exactly. Here's your beads, go out there and start trading! *(Nothing happens.)* There's gold in them thar hills . . .

SGT: Gold? Where? *(Drawing his sword.)*

PADRE: Laguna, do not be guided by greed alone. Else the devil will make you pay for it. Before you know it, you'll be frying in a pan of hot and dirty grease.

SGT: Oh no, sir, bless me. *(He kneels.)* Everything will be done according to the book. The King gets his Royal Fifth and you'll get yours. Yes, gold with which to make your chalice and other holy vessels. Yes, and then I get my fifth! *(Holding a bottle.)*

PADRE: *(As he blesses the beads.)* Remember, although gold is the most precious of all commodities, it is also the means of rescuing souls from hell.

SGT: *(Giving the Padre some coins.)* Does this mean I'll go to heaven?

PADRE: Ahm, this should get you as far as Purgatory.

SINMUHOW: *(Listening in.)* So that's what they're after! It's avarice that brings them to our shores. Under pretext of their so-called religion, they seek the hidden treasures of our land. They die this very night!

TUPIPE: But Sinmuhow, Spirit Woman, they've done no wrong.

SINMUHOW: Silence, don't contradict me! I'll follow him, he makes a lot of noise. You keep an eye on that hypocrite of a priest. *(They all scatter in different directions. At this point there are couples on three different levels.)*

SGT: *(Blindly bumping into Sinmuhow, a blanket around his shoulders, bottle in hand.)* How! How! How . . .

SINMUHOW: How rude!

SGT: You like um wampum? I trade um pretty beads for gold. You got gold?

SINMUHOW: I have no use for your cheap beads.

SGT: What you mean, cheap? Beads worth weight in gold. Wampum.

SINMUHOW: Go peddle your trinkets someplace else.

SGT: Look, why not sell me land. I pay you twenty-four dollars just like Manhattan. I give you Brooklyn Bridge.

SINMUHOW: This land is not for sale. And you can jump off bridge, paleface.

SGT: Why you call me paleface?

SINMUHOW: Cause you gottum face like bucket!

SGT: Oh yeah! Well, just for that, someday we're going to build Coronado Bridge in Logan Heights barrio, yeah, directly over Chicano Park. Then for good measure we build highway patrol substation there. How you like them apples?

SINMUHOW: You speak with forked tongue.

SGT: So, you no like my beads, huh? Okay. What else we trade for gold? How about this nice Meskin blanket, huh? How about this bottle firewater, huh? All Injuns like em drink heap big firewater, dance em rain dance and yell war whoop! *(Sgt. drinks as Sinmuhow seethes.)* Huh, obviously these tactics are not working. *(Combing his hair.)* So, my little Pocahontas, my I have the honor of escorting you to the feast this evening? *(He bows.)* Silence? Why don't we make maize commercial together? No? Hey, I only trying to be nice, ask you out for date. Maybe make you my squaw. Have many little Lagunas. Oh Granma, how can you deny me, Latin Lover Laguna?

SINMUHOW: You stink, don't you ever bathe? We bathe every day.

SGT: *(Losing his patience.)* We use perfume. Come on, where's the God damn gold!

SINMUHOW: Let go of me, honky!

SGT: If you don't tell me where the gold is, I'll break your arm! *(Sinmuhow kicks and flips the Sgt. to the ground.)* Wait, wait . . . I'm part Indian myself! God, I didn't know you knew kung-foo!

CAPITAN: *(On another level.)* Calafia, please listen to me!

SIMQUALE: No! And my name is Simquale-Simquala! Your words are sweet, but your actions are like thorns.

CAPITAN: We wouldn't be happy in my country.

SIMQUALE: Are you ashamed of me, Capitán?

CAPITAN: No, of course not, it's just that certain people wouldn't understand.

SIMQUALE: Then to hell with them and you!

CAPITAN: They wouldn't understand the differences between us, they wouldn't let us live in peace.

SIMQUALE: In what way am I different from you, in what way? In what way?!

CAPITAN: In our features, in our manner, in our thinking. Yet, our hearts are very much alike, Calafia. I swear to you, up there on that mountaintop, all of a sudden I saw what you were trying to tell me. The ways of your people, the meaning of life here. And I saw our hearts, our flesh, mixing together. I had a vision: you see, your people and my people are destined to come together to create a new race of man!

SIMQUALE: There's just one thing, Capitán. And I saw the vision also. Why is it that the Spanish are going to be on top, and my people, the Kemyia, will be on the bottom? Answer that will you! (She exits.)

CAPITAN: Wait, Simquale, wait! We're going to be equals. I swear to you! (Following her.)

PADRE: (On his knees.) Dios! Give me strength! I said, give me strength, Dios. Help us to conquer the diablos, Dios. Yes, there are devils living in this land. We know that Sinmuhow is a consort of Satan!

TUPIPE: Pardon me, sir . . . who are you talking to? (Coming up to him.)

PADRE: Jesus, child . . . you scared the . . . outa me. I was praying to Dios my child, God.

TUPIPE: Oh, where is Dios? I don't see her. Is God the sun or sea or wind or earth?

PADRE: He is all these things, child. Dios is everywhere. See if'n you kin find him in your heart.

TUPIPE: My heart is small, how could Dios fit in there?

PADRE: My little Injun maid, your heart is big as the sky. You have a great capacity to love. I can feel this. So, ask Him to come into your heart, now! Kneel, girl, kneel. Ask Jesús Cristo to come into your little tom-tom right now!

TUPIPE: Who is this . . .

PADRE: (Yanking her down to his level.) Praise the Lord, child! Kneel and pray to Dios. Do like I do, clasp your hands thusly.

TUPIPE: (As though she were playing a game.) Like this?

PADRE: Praise Dios! Throw down your sword and shield, for you shall make war no more, no more!

TUPIPE: How did you know I hated war and killing?

PADRE: My little tomahawk, I know everything! Dios speaks through me. Now lift your head to the sky and sing out his glorious name! No more war, no more hate, no more killing! Hallelujah! Repeat after me! Hallelujah!

TUPIPE: HALLELUJAH!

PADRE: HALLELUJAH!

BOTH: HAAAALLEEEEEEEELUUUUUUUJAAAAHHHH!

TUPIPE: Oh, that sent chills up and down my spine!

PADRE: There, you see. Dios has taken possession of your body! Praise the Lord! (*Standing up, he dances with her.*) We gonna dance for joy! Yah! Uah! We gonna dance for joy!

TUPIPE: Wait a minute, what are you doing?

PADRE: I'm gonna save your soul, girl.

TUPIPE: My soul . . .

PADRE: Your soul. It may be too late to save them other witches, but you are still young. Yes, you are like virgin gold, uncorrupted and pure. Now then, are you ready to receive Dios? Are you ready to take him into your soul? First you must confess and forsake your pagan ways. Cast aside your sins!

TUPIPE: I've committed no sins!

PADRE: Have your sisters committed sins, are they thinking of committing sins?

TUPIPE: No, no!

PADRE: You're lying, I can see it in your eyes. Tell me the truth.

TUPIPE: Why do I have to listen to you? Who are you anyway?

PADRE: I am the voice of God! There is evil in this land! Cleanse yourself, now!

TUPIPE: The only evil is you and your kind. Get out now while you have the chance! Otherwise we'll kill you!

PADRE: Oh wickedness, Oh viciousness! Drive these evil thoughts from your mind, right now! Renounce Satan, renounce Sinmuhow!

TUPIPE: I'm telling you for the last time! Leave now or be put to death!

PADRE: No, killing is murder and murder is sin and sin is eternal damnation!

TUPIPE: I don't want to be the one to kill you! So leave now, while there is still time! Please! (*She cries.*)

PADRE: (*He comforts her.*) My little peace pipe, embrace me! I see that you have the heart of a true Christian!

TUPIPE: I don't want to hurt a soul!

PADRE: Let God's love douse the bitter flames of hate. I say, do you feel Him growing inside of you?

TUPIPE: Is God a man? (*They embrace.*)

PADRE: Yes, he is the Father of us all. And he is about to enter your spirit! I now baptize you Ramona, after the famous novel yet to be written, in the name of the Father and of the Son and of the Holy Ghost!

TUPIPE: *(Struggling like a wildcat as he restrains her.)* My name is Tupipe-Tunan!

PADRE: You gots to have a Christian name! My first convert! This must be a sign. This spot is sacred! I, Padre Junípero de La Jolla Serra do hereby establish La Sagrada Misión de San Diego de Alcalá in this year of our Lord, 1769! *(Dragging Tupipe away with him.)* Come on, Ramona!

CAPITAN: *(On the other side of the stage with Sgt.)* Sgt. Laguna! What happened to you? Where's your pants, your sword?

SGT: I was attacked by the Amazons, hundreds of them. They beat me and stole my beads and clothes. I fought the best I could, slew dozens, but they won the day by sheer force of numbers.

CAPITAN: Laguna, have you been drinking again?

SGT: Yes, but by God, I tell you there is danger here! Let us quit this place and sail back to Spain at once.

PADRE: *(Entering, adjusting his clothes.)* Mi Capitán, the Sgt. is right. I just gained the confidence of the girl, her name is Ramona now. She warned me that an attack is imminent! But I say we take the offensive . . . slay the Medicine Woman and take the Queen prisoner. Then we have the whole tribe by the throat!

CAPITAN: You speak foolishly and wild! I myself have been with Calafia all day. Once more, we are in love and propose to unite our lives and fortunes in holy matrimony this very night!

SINMUHOW: *(On the other side of the stage.)* Tupipe-Tunan! Where have you been?

TUPIPE: In the woods with the Padre, picking wildflowers.

SINMUHOW: Picking wildflowers! You play while your tribe is in mortal danger! You know there is an attack being planned. Go and get your arms. Wait, come back, why are you crying? What is this around your neck?

TUPIPE: A rosary!

SINMUHOW: More beads! *(Ripping them off.)* Speak, what is the matter with you?

TUPIPE: Oh Sinmuhow, he baptized me and made me pray to his God. And then he . . . he, I hate him! I hate him!

SINMUHOW: Here comes your sister! Tell her of this! *(Enter Simquale.)*

CAPITAN: I'm going to parley with them, there will be no more fighting!

SGT: I'll bring up the rear. *(Keeping out of harm's way.)*

PADRE: And I'll go and pray for peace. *(Exit.)*

SINMUHOW: *(To Simquale.)* Marry him and it will mark the death of us.

SIMQUALE: *(To Capitán.)* The Padre dishonored my sister! I want his head!

CAPITAN: That's not the way to do things! *(As Capitán and Simquale argue, Padre unexpectedly runs into Tupipe and Sinmuhow.)*

TUPIPE: It's him! It's the Padre!

SINMUHOW: Slay him! *(As they both run Padre through.)*

PADRE: I only baptized her! *(Padre falls as Sgt. happens upon the scene, then exits, running.)*

SIMQUALE: You had better make good your word this time, Capitán. *(Exiting to join her sisters.)*

SGT: Mi Capitán! Mi Capitán! They've killed the good Padre La Jolla. He was a peaceful man. I saw it with my own eyes. They laid hold of him as a wolf would lay hold of a lamb and tore his Holy habit off, gave him blows with their clubs and discharged countless arrows into his body. Not content with that, they beat and cut to pieces his face, head and the whole of his body, so that nothing remained except for his consecrated hands, which I found intact, in the place where he was murdered!

CAPITAN: Simquale! Simquale! *(Coming fast upon the women with his sword drawn.)* I told you I would police my own! But now that you have taken matters into your own hands, I demand her head *(Pointing to Sinmuhow.)* in exchange for the life of our Holy Father!

SIMQUALE: You shall not touch her!

CAPITAN: Simquale! *(Trying to kill Sinmuhow, he slays Simquale.)* My beloved!

SINMUHOW: Death to the Spanish! *(A battle ensues. The Sgt. slays Sinmuhow but Tupipe shoots an arrow through the Sgt. Then Tupipe fights hand to hand with the Capitán, who beats her to the ground.)*

CAPITAN: *(Holding a knife to her throat.)* Salvaje! Stop! I will spare your life on one condition: you lay down your arms and fight no more. *(Letting her rise.)* There has been enough bloodshed here.

TUPIPE: My people, we are half as many as we once were. Where are the Kemyia?

CAPITAN: From now on you shall be called Diegueños, after San Diego, in memory of the slain Padre who was attacked and killed here in La Misión de San Diego de Alcalá, 1775. Get to work!

TUPIPE: You treat us like animals. *(She labors.)*

CAPITAN: From now on, all unmarried women and girls over the age of nine will be locked up.

TUPIPE: We cannot live like this. The women's quarters are only seven by two feet per person, barely enough space to sleep in, inadequately ventilated, filthy!

CAPITAN: Do not complain or you shall be whipped!

TUPIPE: You may have beaten us, but you shall not make slaves of our children! We shall practice abortion and infanticide!

CAPITAN: Wait, what are you doing?

TUPIPE: Can't you see? I'm dying . . .

CAPITAN: Smallpox! *(Reviving her.)* This has gone too far. Don't die! We'll give you your lands back! It's 1834! We're part of the newly formed Republic of Mexico! The mission system is abolished! Slavery is abolished! ¡Afuera con Los Gachupines! ¡Viva México!

TUPIPE: You keep the best lands for yourself, you still exploit us. *(She rises to his level.)*

CAPITAN: But we intermarried with your people as we did in Mexico.

TUPIPE: Always holding the Spanish side of your heritage in higher esteem than ours.

CAPITAN: *(Embracing her as his wife.)* Querida, what difference does it make now? Those bad times are past. The year is 1840 and we're all Mexican citizens, Cristianos as well. And nuestros hijos are white, black, brown, all colors . . . like the rainbow. Even the Governor of California, Pío Pico, is a mulatto.

TUPIPE: But he claims he's Spanish, gente de razón.

CAPITAN: Ah! Money whitens. You know, only one thing bothers me. We never did find that gold spoken of in the myth, Calafia's gold.

SGT: *(Entering with Sinmuhow as his wife dressed as a Miner '49er.)* Did someone mention the word gold!

CAPITAN: Who are you, how did you get here?

SGT: I'm a gold miner, '49er, and this is darlin' Clementine. We walked over the Rocky Mountains.

CAPITAN: Then, welcome Señor, mi casa es su casa.

SGT: Why thank you. I like this house very much. I'm going to enjoy living here.

CAPITAN: And what is your mission? Why have you come here?

SGT: Gold, for one thing . . .

CAPITAN: Oh, you won't find any around here!

SGT: And destiny for another!

ALL: But that's another story! *(All six actors are on stage now, three dressed like Yankees, three like Californios. The finale consists of a dance. A Yankee couple waltzes, a Californio couple does a corrida.*

The Yankees square dance, the Californios fandango. At first the competition is friendly but gradually the dances turn more and more aggressive. Two cultures in conflict, the dancers close in a tableau of incomprehension, competition, combat.)

El Jardín
An Acto

CHARACTERS

DIOS *(Also plays Cristóbal Colón.)*
EVA
ADAN *(Also plays Taíno.)*
LA SERPIENTE *(Also plays Matón, Padre Ladrón and Muerte.)*

SCENES

Paradise, Hell and Earth

DIOS: *(At rise.)* Soy la voz de Dios. I am the voice of God. I have been speaking to mis hijos since the first hombre appeared in the universe. His name was Adán and he lived in El Jardín with a woman named Eva who was somewhat of a coquette. Do you remember?

ADAN: *(In the garden.)* So, you've been talking con ese serpent again, eh?

EVA: Sí pues, so what!

ADAN: You should be ashamed of yourself!

EVA: Oh, he's not so bad.

ADAN: What do you mean, tonta, he's evil!

EVA: But he has such a nice slick body. He's soooo ssssslimmmmy!

ADAN: *(Making the sign of the cross.)* ¡Madre mía! My God, woman, don't you know you should judge a person by his spirit?

EVA: Well, I'm more inclined towards the flesh.

ADAN: I'm going to tell you something woman. I catch that snake in the grass around here again, I'm going to wring it around your neck!

EVA: Oh, the way he slides and slithers on the ground . . . he's sooooooooooo evil.

ADAN: How can you be such a pendeja? Don't you know he'll lead you into temptation?

EVA: He says he wants to teach me about life, about knowledge.

ADAN: Eva, you're going to get us evicted from El Jardín!

EVA: So what, I'm tired of all that jive the man's been laying down on you. Just look at this place, tame tigers, obnoxious little lambs, I feel like I'm in some kind of zoo. Hey, I want a little action. I want to swing, baby. How come we never go dancing?

ADAN: Now just a minute! We're not prisoners here. We can leave any time we want. We have free will. Dios has been very kind to us and under no circumstances do I want to incur his wrath.

EVA: Oh, let him kick us out . . . see if he can find two other suckers to take our place!

ADAN: Are you out of your mind? You want to give up El Jardín?
        The rent is free, the air is clean
        We got no barrios, got no machines
        No one gets rich, no one eats crumbs
        We don't need money and we don't drop bombs
        We got peace, we got love
        We got Dios, we got enough

There's the sun, there's the sea
Here is heaven and here are we
We got the lambs, we got the grass
We are all brothers, there is no class

All creation blends real nice
In the center of Paradise.

EVA: That's just it, we're no better than *worms* to Him!

ADAN: Or *whales* for that matter! En los ojos de Dios we are all equal!

EVA: Oh, that rap about equality and justice is like a tired old psalm. Listen brother, if we really had freedom in this here cage we'd be able to come and go as we pleased. Why can't we take a trip or a vacation?

ADAN: Eva, I don't want to go anywhere! I happen to like it here.

EVA: Well I'm bored! I'm stagnating, I'm not satisfied!

ADAN: Eva, don't be crazy . . .

EVA: All day long I sit around and hear the birds go "tweet, tweet, tweet" and the lambs go "baa, baaa, baaaa!" I want to do something, go shopping, anything. Look at me, I'm naked, I don't have any clothes!

ADAN: Now I know you're really flipped out! What do you need clothes for? You're beautiful just the way you are.

EVA: Maybe some jewelry, or just a nice hat. Do you really think I am beautiful?

ADAN: Just look at yourself in this gentle pool . . . come closer. See your reflection in the liquid mirror . . . your bronze skin . . . your long black hair.

EVA: I am beautiful, aren't I?

ADAN: You are the most beautiful woman in the entire universe.

EVA: Of course I am! I'm the only woman in the universe. Don't try to flatter me!

ADAN: Eva, querida, just think, you are the only one, you are perfect, you are His creation.

DIOS: *(Voice from above.)* ¡Hola! ¡Hola! What's going on down there?

ADAN: Nothing, jefe, we were just having a discussion.

DIOS: It sounded like you were shouting. It sounded like disharmony.

ADAN: Oh no sir, we were only reviewing our theology.

DIOS: Good, any points you want clarified?

ADAN: No sir, we know it very well.

DIOS: Very good, "In the beginning . . ." *(Voice fades.)*

EVA: "In the beginning, there was nothing . . ." Just what is that supposed to mean?

ADAN: Exactly what it says. Before Him there was nada, then He came and there was todo.

EVA: But where did he come from?

ADAN: He has always been here and He will always be here.

EVA: But it doesn't make any *sense.*

ADAN: It is the word of God!

EVA: Oh brother, that's another thing that bugs the *hell* out of me.

ADAN: Don't say that word!

EVA: There's no free speech in El Jardín!

ADAN: Shut up! Don't you say another word!

EVA: Why can't I have an apple?

ADAN: Keep your voice down!

EVA: I'm tired of eating nothing! Why can't I have some carne asada and some hot salsa with frijoles and arroz? I'd even settle for a hamburger with french fries. Or a Tequila Sunrise!

ADAN: The serpent promised you all those things!

EVA: He said I could start with dessert.

ADAN: You keep away from there!

EVA: Such a silly rule about a stupid tree.

ADAN: Eva, that's the only rule He has laid down. Now, why he doesn't want us eating the Fruit of the Forbidden Tree is none of my concern.

EVA: Don't you see! He's the big ranchero. We're nothing but peons!

ADAN: For the last time, I'm telling you, I feel great satisfaction living in peace with my fellow creatures. I have no desire to eat them or wear their hides. Why are you so ungrateful? Don't you love me anymore?

EVA: Yes, I love you, te quiero mucho. But it is only a love between brother and sister. I want to love you more, I want to love all of you!

ADAN: *(Crossing himself.)* Oh my Dios! En el nombre del Padre, el Hijo, el Espíritu Santo . . .

EVA: Why are you blushing?

ADAN: You make me think sinful thoughts.

EVA: Hmmmmmmmmm. Tell me about them. I want to know it all.

ADAN: No, it's time for my, uh, Bible Study class. See you later!
    (Adán runs out covering his private parts.)

EVA: No, don't go, stay here with your Mamasota!

Why can't I have my way
Why do I have to stay
Here in the green Jardín

Sure it's a calm place
Larks sing, gazelles race
It hardly rains at all
Fruit from the trees do fall
Creatures both large and small
Love one and they love all
We always sleep late
Angels guard the gate
It never gets cold here
Nothing can be sold here

But I need more than this
More than complacency
Or smug security
I want to dance, I want to shout
I want to leap, I want to fly out
But more than wanting to go
Most important, I want to know

SERPIENTE: *(Enters accompanied by flutes and drums.)* Dig it!

EVA: Ayyyyy, un monster!

SERPIENTE: ¡Qué monster ni que mi abuela! You just don't appreciate style and class. I'm Coco Roco, indigenous down to my alligator-skinned huaraches.

EVA: But you look so feo.

SERPIENTE: Bah! That's the trouble with you hyphenated Mexicans, you can't appreciate other cultures.

EVA: I'm no hyphenated Mexican-American. ¡Yo soy Chicana!

SERPIENTE: ¡Tu madre!

EVA: ¡La tuya que está en vinagre!

SERPIENTE: *(Strutting around, sizing her up.)* Huh, let's check this chick out.

EVA: I'm not a "chick," I'm a mujer. Don't look at me like that, you feathered iguana.

SERPIENTE: Baby, I'm just admiring you in all your perfect innocence.

EVA: Don't touch me, resbaloso.

SERPIENTE: What's the matter, mamacita, don't you dig my movida?

EVA: I guess I have to get used to you. Last time you were just a little snake.

SERPIENTE: I have many faces, you'll see. In this life I am Coco Roco. Fire flames from my mouth and smoke seeps from my ears. The horns at the top of my head are the horns of the bull of fertility and here behind me is the tail of sensuality. My body is made up of the earth which is rich and brown and gives life to all. This girdle of live snakes wound round my middle is further proof of my power of lust . . .

EVA: You're just too much . . .

SERPIENTE: Be careful one of my little snakes doesn't escape and slip into you!

EVA: You beast!

SERPIENTE: You love it!

EVA: Get out of here before I squash you!

SERPIENTE: You don't understand, you don't appreciate me, do you Eva? That's because you are a white woman living under the European God and your mind is poisoned by their treacherous white ways!

EVA: That's not true, I'm a mestiza, and I'm proud of it.

SERPIENTE: You live in Paradise, worshiping the Lord who will one day come with the conquistadores of España, the bearded ones, and you will be La Malinche, she who will interpret for the white man and betray your own tribe, tu raza. You will even mate with their leader, Hernán Cortés, and the first of a bastard race will be born in Tenochtitlán-México!

EVA: You're lying, I don't believe this will happen.

SERPIENTE: (Aside.) She doesn't think I can see into the future. Well, I'll have to show her a little preview of history. Eva, come here . . . do you see that planet way down there?

EVA: What, I don't see anything.

SERPIENTE: The clouds are obscuring your sight, blow them away.

EVA: Oh yes, I see it now, it's blue and green.

SERPIENTE: That's earth. Now focus off the eastern coast of Mexico to a small island in the Caribbean. The year is 1492. Do you see? (On the opposite side of the stage enter Taíno and Cristóbal Colón.)

EVA: Who are those men?

SERPIENTE: The man with the flag in his hand is Cristóbal Colón. The other man, scantily dressed, is a native of the island. His name is Borinquen the Taíno. Can you hear what they are saying?

COLON: Y nosotros tomamos posesión de estas tierras en el nombre del Rey de España . . .

TAINO: (Circling Colón, puzzled.) Caribe? Maya? Seminole?

COLON: Y Santo sea el nombre de Dios, Vuestro Rey.

TAINO: Aztec? Toltec? Chichimec? Zapotec?

COLON: ¿Qué estupideces tratais de decirnos?

TAINO: Inca! Inca! No? Illinois! Ohio! Ute! Indiana! (Laughing at "Indiana.")

COLON: ¡Chingueis tu madreis, imbécileis!

TAINO: Ahhhhaaaaa! Polynesia. Malasia. Asia. China? Chop chop?

COLON: ¡No, no, no! España, Europa. Yo Espania. ¡Tu indio, indio!

TAINO: ¿Indio? No. Noooooo. Taíno. Taíno. Borinquen. (Motioning to the land around him.) Borinquen.

COLON: No, indio tonto. Esta es La India. Tu eres indio. Esta isla se llama Puerto Rico. ¿Comprende? (Speaking very slowly as though he were speaking to a brute.)

TAINO: (Shrugging his shoulders, he offers Colón some fruit and tobacco.) ¡Ummmmm, guayaba! ¡Banana! ¡Tobaco!

COLON: Hmmmmmmmm. Muy bien. Okay! (Indicates he is tired after the meal.) ¿Hotel? ¿Hotel?

TAINO: ¿Hotel? ¡No, hotel no! (Taíno points across ocean indicating Colón should return from whence he came.) Caribe, bye bye, adiós!

COLON: Espera, amigo. Ahora que ustedes son los sujetos de Su Majestad, será necesario encontrar empleo. (Breaking into a southern accent.) I think we going to lay down the Plaza de Armas down there . . .

TAINO: ¿Que qué? ¡Espera, acabo de aprender el español!

COLON: We'll put the church up here and the Embassy over there.

TAINO: Ahora, qué estás talking?

COLON: Muy bueno, amigo, you learn pronto. Lookee here, you Injuns will provide manual labor, us Europeans boss man.

TAINO: Manual labor? Lo conozco. He lives in the same housing project as me.

COLON: Amigo, after the conquest . . .

TAINO: Which one?

COLON: After the colonization, after we put in the freeways, from Corpus Christi to San Francisco, after we put in the Taco Bells with that distinct Spanish architecture, we will have created a great civilization, you and I . . . a monument of cooperation among two culturas, what do you say?

TAINO: Sounds great, when do we start?

COLON: Right now. The church has to go up first. We'll pay you five coconuts per day.

TAINO: Five cocos a day . . . that's not a decent living wage!

COLON: Pardner, we ain't even conquered this place yet. We got a high overhead and a low yield for the first few fiscal centuries.

TAINO: But my Raza, we will all starve to death.

COLON: We'll just have to import 2,000 Mau Maus from Africa to finish the job.

TAINO: No, we will not do it, for it is slavery! We shall resist.

COLON: We got a law says you'll not agitate to form a seditious union.

TAINO: You're going to have to build your city over my dead body! (*Taking up arms.*)

COLON: That's okay with me, boy. Here, have some whiskey. Here, have some gin. Have some smallpox. Have some tuberculosis! Boy, I really love you all, your spirit, your love of the land, you proud and noble savage you! Why, I'm part Injun myself!

TAINO: (*About to strike Colón down.*) Death to the Europeans!

COLON: (*Pulling out a crucifix.*) Behold! Behold! The mighty cross of our Lord, Jesus Christ! Kneel, bow your knees. Feel the power of our Master!

TAINO: (*On his knees.*) I am your slave! (*Lights out on Taíno-Colón.*)

SERPIENTE: So you see, Eva, the Europeans will use God's name to conquer our people and there will be centuries of oppression. And your people, Eva, your brown-skinned Raza, will live their days scratching out a meager existence on earth for the false promise of a glorious place in heaven.

EVA: Dios promised us that the meek would inherit the earth.

SERPIENTE: Only the dirt, Eva, only the miserable dirt of poverty.

EVA: What can I do to prevent this from happening?

SERPIENTE: Eat of the fruit of the Tree of Knowledge.

EVA: Tell me more!

SERPIENTE: Under the light of the skull-white moon
> In the barrios of ancient Aztlán
> A pyramid lies, as tall as the sky
> There on the temple grounds
> Amidst the steaming rites
> There on the sacred stone
> There with my golden knife
> I will slash the holy fruit
> There with my bloody blade
> I will eat your tender heart

EVA: Are you going to do all that to me?! (*Sexually stimulated, en-*

thralled.)

SERPIENTE: I was only speaking metaphorically, don't take me so literally.

EVA: That's what I like about you: you're so intellectual.

SERPIENTE: We have built our temples tall
                Hidden deep in barrio steam
                They will measure most precisely
                What we seek in mescal dreams
                In our spacious astral minds
                Lies a universe that gleams
                Like the cosmos high above
                With its stars of crystalline

EVA: Ay, ay, ay!

SERPIENTE: Shall we go to my altar on the Pyramid of Coco Roco?

EVA: Is it far from here?

SERPIENTE: Only through the Doubting Peaks and into the Valley of the Fascinating Fog! *(They exit. Enter Dios and Adán from opposite side walking arm in arm.)*

ADAN: Dios, I don't know what to do about Eva . . . she's so hard-headed.

DIOS: I know, I made her that way. I fear it will grow to be a trait. You, on the other hand, are much more level-headed. Although I fear you will have a propensity for baldness. Darn it, nothing is perfect! Hey, is it my imagination or are you getting taller?

ADAN: No sir, my dimensions are from heaven to earth and from the west to the east as you have decreed.

DIOS: You're so big for your age. It's hard to believe that you are only a few days old. You know, I just started creating this world last Monday. Here it is Saturday. You and Eva were one of my last projects. Maybe I'll take a day off tomorrow.

ADAN: Dios, what am I going to do with Eva? She's not happy.

DIOS: Unhappy! In Paradise? Impossible! That I can't believe. Huh. See those mountains over there? Don't they look rather crooked? Let me landscape them with a little more finesse. *(He waves his hands and transforms them.)* And look at that river, I think I'll change its color. By the way, did you walk the unicorn this morning?

ADAN: Wow!

DIOS: Maybe Eva needs a change. How about if I make her shorter, fatter, and darker?

ADAN: No, I like her just the way she is, thank you, in spite of any

113

faults. You see, she's like a different side of me.

DIOS: How strange, I never saw it that way. I, for one, have always been the Father, the Son and the Holy Ghost. Say, isn't your nose rather large? Would you like a smaller one?

ADAN: No, no, it's fine the way it is. Let me tell you more about Eva, she keeps talking about the "kid," the "kid."

DIOS: What "kid?" You mean the goat?

ADAN: No, she speaks of "the kid of our creation."

DIOS: The kid of your creation. That could only mean one thing. She means to bear fruit! But how, if both of you are innocent? Is there something you haven't told me?

ADAN: She says that if she eats of the Fruit of the Forbidden Tree she will also bear fruit!

DIOS: She's been talking to La Serpiente. I see it all now! That snake has tricked Eva into going down to earth with him. They are on top of a pyramid together!

ADAN: My God, you've got to stop her! Let's go, where's my angel wings? . . . shall we take the elevator?

DIOS: No Adán, I can't help you. This is between Eva and her conscience. Fly quickly!

ADAN: I'll be back. (*Depending on the cleverness of the set designer, Adán can either leap down a trap door on stage or jump into a pile of trash off stage creating a loud din.*)

DIOS: ¡Vaya con Dios! (*Sitting down on a cloud, dejectedly.*) Jeeez, maybe I should have posted an archangel or something to guard that damn tree!

SERPIENTE: (*Down below, Eva lies prone atop the pyramid. The Serpiente stands over her with a knife in his hand.*)

> Is not this tuna red and ripe
> Something to want to make you bite
> Into the juices of your brain
> Suck out creation, go insane

EVA: ¡Ay, ay, ay! ¡Qué locura!

SERPIENTE: Would you not like to masticate
> Forbidden fruit at this late date
> Ingest your mind with this explosion
> Blast off from heaven into motion

EVA: ¡Dime más, dime más!

SERPIENTE: Chicana, hembra, woman of the sun, my uh . . . (*Straining for images.*) your skin reflects the beauty of that bronze star! May, uh, my golden knife . . . mate with your brown body!

EVA: What are you going to do, loco?

SERPIENTE: Cut the tuna.

EVA: But it's such a beautiful tuna, so red, so ripe.

SERPIENTE: Stay still, this won't hurt a bit. *(Shrill, strident music is heard.)*

EVA: Noooooooooooooooooo! *(Serpiente cuts into the tuna.)*

SERPIENTE: Ummmmmmmmm. This tuna tastes real good. Wanna bite?

EVA: Golly, I don't know.

SERPIENTE: I knew it, you still got religion.

EVA: I better go, Adán is going to be real mad at me.

SERPIENTE: That Jesus freak! He doesn't have the balls to eat this!

EVA: He does so! *(She grabs the tuna out of his hand.)* Anyway, what's so special about this fruit?

SERPIENTE: Have they kept everything from you, my little torta? This is the fruit of the Tree of Knowledge. Eat it and you will be injected with all the wisdom of the ages. Not only that, my little enchilada, you will soon learn to deduct and deduce, thereby gaining corporate control of corporal beings.

EVA: I'm not interested in that corporate control stuff, I seek knowledge.

SERPIENTE: My little quesadilla, once you discover the wheel, you'll have the mechanics to build a marvelous civilization.

EVA: Will my people acknowledge this? Will women be appreciated? *(Thunder and lightening build in intensity.)*

SERPIENTE: My little jalapeño, you will be worshiped, idolized, put on pedestals! Take a bite!

EVA: Will I create? *(The sky darkens, wind blows fiercely.)*

SERPIENTE: My little chile pepper, you will create zillions of men and women just as Dios did in his image! Bite it!

EVA: *(Sustained drum roll, Eva bites into it.)* Ohhhhhhhh . . .

SERPIENTE: You did it, my little fajita! You did it! ¡Cuidado, tiene espinas!

EVA: Ouch, it has thorns!

SERPIENTE: That's right, my little taco belle, along with the good comes the bad. And I am the baaaaaaaad. Make no mistake about that!

EVA: ¡Dios mío! I see it all now, you are the devil! *(Thunder, lightening, drenching rain.)*

SERPIENTE: Sí, mujer, I am el mentiroso, el atascado, el borracho, el asesino! ¡SOY EL GRAN PUTO!

EVA: What have I done
              My mind is reeling
              And heaven is wheeling away
              I feel suspended in space
              And chastity flees from my face
              Paradise seems far away
              And earth 'neath my feet bids me to stay
              For many years and many days
              To spend my life in toil and waste
              In weeding gardens, cleaning cribs
              And needling for Grace

SERPIENTE: *(As Adán enters.)*
              Here comes your man from heaven
              To join you here on Earth
              Why don't you talk him into
              Sharing your worldly berth
              As for me, I must flee
              See you in a century *(Exit Serpiente.)*

ADAN: Mi chavalona, why?

EVA: I ate the apple, I sure did
              My heart is thumping, it sure is
              My knees are shaking, they sure are
              My head is rocking to the stars
              But I can see much clearer now
              The earth seems much more dearer now

ADAN: You don't know what you're saying there
              Your eyes are flying everywhere
              There's nothing dear about the land
              Nothing but work for all us men
              Why should we leave the promised land
              The home of tigers and of lambs

EVA: Baby, eat this red ripe fruit
              Swear to God, it makes you shoot
              Take a bite, it tastes real good
              Eat it honey, wish you would

ADAN: You little fool, you've cast us out
              of El Jardín where we devout
              Had lived an ageless loving life
              Without death, without cruel strife

EVA: Adán, eat it . . . if you love me!

ADAN: To join her in her cursed state

A life of whim, a life of fate
To leave all that I loved behind
To join the wheel and low and whine
A bigger fool is he than she
To eat from the Forbidden tree
(Adán takes a bite, chokes.)

EVA: Adán, cuidado, it has thorns! *(Adán howls in pain.)* Oh, my darling, are they stuck in your throat? I'm afraid you'll never get them out!

ADAN: ¡Me espiné! I should have never listened to you! Get me a drink of water!

EVA: *(Suddenly, we hear the sounds of civilization, autos, radios, etc.)* Oh my God . . . this stream . . . it's polluted! *(Garbage is thrown on stage.)*

ADAN: What are you doing running around naked? Go put something on!

EVA: Adán, that never bothered you before!

ADAN: Well, it upsets me now! So go and dress yourself!

EVA: *(Eva puts on a skirt and hands Adán some pants.)* Very well. Here, don't you think you ought to practice some modesty?

ADAN: And cook something for me, I'm hungry.

EVA: There's nothing to eat, I'm afraid, but the rest of this apple. *(Eva munches on the apple.)* You know, it's rather cold down here.

ADAN: Look, there's a cave we can sleep in! Go and gather wood for a fire.

EVA: Can't you say please!

ADAN: Vieja, ¡no me agüites! Don't give me a hard time! *(As they gather firewood, Dios appears on a cloud above.)*

DIOS: ¡Hola! Can you hear me?

ADAN: Of course, Dios, how are you?

DIOS: Fine, it's Sunday, you know, and I was just watching the Northern Lights on my sky screen.

ADAN: Dios, I know this is supposed to be a day of rest, but I've got to get this work done before dark.

EVA: Adán, who are you talking to?

ADAN: Shhhh, don't interrupt, can't you hear, I'm talking to Dios.

EVA: I can't hear Him.

ADAN: Dios, I think Eva and I are going to have a baby!

DIOS: Well, uh, have fun, and, uh, watch out for the dinosaurs.

EVA: Where . . . where is His voice coming from?

DIOS: Adán, tell Eva that from now on she will have to speak to me through you.

ADAN: Eva, you must speak to Him through me.

EVA: No, don't say that . . . it's not true!

DIOS: "In pain she shall bring forth children, yet her desire shall be for her husband and he shall rule over her."

ADAN: I will do as you command, my Lord. But will we ever see you again?

DIOS: Perhaps someday I shall send down my son . . .

EVA: Dios, Diosito, por favor, please . . . talk to me!

DIOS: (As he walks over to a cross.) To be crucified!

ADAN: Silence woman! You will be quiet! (Forcing Eva down on her knees.) Pray, pray for forgiveness!

SERPIENTE: (Entering with a whip, rope.) You see, ever since that day, la mujer no vale madre, woman ain't worth shit. Hey don't get mad! This was before the advent of feminism. (As he lashes Dios to the cross.) Now then, it's time to celebrate my victory. Come here Christian, and turn the other cheek.

ADAN: (Like a priest before the altar.)
After millions of years Dios will send his son
A shepherd who leads his flock to safety
But there in Calvary the people will turn against him
And the father shall sacrifice his only son
So with the shedding of His blood
We will be saved from damnation

ADAN: (With Eva kneeling beside him.)
The spirit is free and ethereal
It hangs suspended between heaven and earth
It is the uplifting of humanity
Giving life the will to rise
It is man's life buoy
To which he must cleave after death

(Satanic music. Dios is crucified, He screams, the Serpent laughs, darkness, except for a follow spot on Serpent.)

SERPIENTE: And so, Adán and Eva escaped El Jardín and settled down to a glorious existence on Earth. Besides fratricide, genocide and infanticide, there have been holy wars, class wars, and gas wars. You mortals have fueled the fires of Hades and entered my domain with bloody smiles on your Aztec faces. And what today? There's Adán and Eva living in middle class comfort in Chicago, Illinois. Isn't that the American Dream? (Lights up on Adán and Eva's living room, furnished right out of the Sears &

Roebuck catalog. Enter Adán, dejectedly, dressed in a white shirt and tie, sport coat over his shoulder, Wall Street Journal *in hand. This could be the start of any sit-com on T.V.)*

EVA: *(Voice, off stage.)* Adam, honey, is that you?

ADAN: Yes, dear.

EVA: *(Entering, dressed in an apron and blonde wig.)* How was your day at the office? *(Adán does not answer.)* Would you like a cocktail, dear?

ADAN: Yes, I could use one.

EVA: *(Picking up a can of ready-made drink.)* Black Russian or Tequila Sunrise?

ADAN: Whatever.

EVA: *(Opening the can and handing it to him.)* Now then, what would you like for din-din? Swedish, Chinese, Pakistani or Polynesian? And then, there's always Mexican.

ADAN: I had Mexican for lunch. Let's go with . . . oh, whatever you want. *(Mumbling under his breath.)* It all tastes the same anyway.

EVA: No problem, I'll just pop it in the microwave. Thank God for Stouffer's. So, how's the stock market? Did you make some good commissions today?

ADAN: Let's talk about your day, dear.

EVA: Well, after I tidied up a bit I watched "General Hospital." Holly foiled Oliver's attempt to kill Luke, but Oliver reported back to Basil that Luke and Holly are both in love with that geologist, Mr. Harper.

ADAN: Luke is in love with Mr. Harper?

EVA: Yes, he's really a transsexual with only one gonad! Isn't that a scream! Oh, but this is so silly. Wait until I tell you the good news. Honey, I am going to be a part-time Mary Kay rep and sell enough cosmetics to help pay for our hot tub! Isn't that wonderful! I could even win a pink Volvo. *(Adán is very quiet.)* Adam, is something wrong?

ADAN: Eve, I lost my job. I am no longer an account executive for Ferner, Ferner, Farmer and Fudd. They gave me my two weeks notice!

EVA: But Adam, weren't you selling more CD's and SL's than any AE? Weren't you bullish on bonds and bearish on . . .

ADAN: Haven't you been watching the news? We're in the middle of a severe recession. Everybody's cutting back. And the latest hired are the first to be fired.

EVA: Don't worry, Adam, you'll find another job.

ADAN: Fat chance! The unemployment rate is the highest since the Great Depression. Eve, we could lose this house!

EVA: Oh Adam, we can't let that happen. That's what we worked for all our lives. All those years of schooling, losing our accents, leaving the barrio!

ADAN: Chin-gow! Why didn't I wait until the interest rates went down before I signed the mortgage note?

EVA: Adam, we'll make it somehow. I'll go to work full time for Mary Kay.

ADAN: Who's going to buy cosmetics when they can't even afford groceries?

EVA: I'll sell Amway products. Better yet, I'll sell the Cambridge Diet. Even fat people have to eat!

ADAN: Jesus, what are we going to do? You work for something all your life and it comes crashing down on you in one day! *(The doorbell rings.)*

EVA: Now, who could that be? *(Enter Matón, dressed in a suit and tie, very professional, with briefcase and calling card. He also wears a pair of dark glasses.)*

MATON: You don't know me. My name is Mr. Matón. Mind if I come into your cantón?

ADAN: *(Exchanging cards with Matón.)* Adam Martinez, formerly with Ferner, Ferner, Farmer and Fudd. This is my wife, Eve.

MATON: Sorry to hear that you lost your position, Mr. Martinez, but I have a product here you might be interested in purchasing. It's called "Sabe."

EVA: "Sabe?" Sounds like an underarm deodorant. Excuse me, haven't we met before?

MATON: *(Ignoring her.)* "Sabe" comes from the word, "saber," which means to have knowledge. Are you Chicanos?

ADAN: Mr. Matón, my wife and I aren't into playing little ethnic games. We are American, Mexican-American. And what do I need "Sabe" for?

MATON: You need "Sabe" because the Gringos have taken it away from you. Don't you see? They have not only stolen our land, they have stolen our culture and claimed it as their own. *(Sarcastically, with an Anglo accent.)* Chile con carne, buckaroo, adobe houses, Taco Bells! Take "Sabe" and this will all be given back to you. Now tell me, why do you think you lost your job?

ADAN: Economic factors; in spite of falling interest rates, the Consumer Price Index has risen. Also, tight money factors by the Fed.

MATON: ¡Puro pedo! You know the real reason why you lost your job. *(Pulling a mirror out of his briefcase.)*

ADAN: No, no.

MATON: Yes, yes, it's because of that. *(Showing him the mirror.)*

EVA: What is it? Is that "Sabe?"

MATON: You lost your job because you are a Mexican! The only reason they hired you in the first place was because of Affirmative Action. But now, all that has ended!

EVA: Oh, what rubbish!

MATON: Do you really think that just because you dress and act and eat and talk like them, they will accept you? Nel, look at your face, it's brown! *(The mirror is having a hypnotic effect upon Adán.)*

ADAN: How is "Sabe" supposed to help me?

MATON: By making you aware of what you are and giving you the huevos to do something about it. With extra strength "Sabe," we can beat the Gringo.

ADAN: All right, give it to me, I'll try it. What have I got to lose?

MATON: *(Pulling out a bomb from his briefcase, Eva shrieks.)* Here it is, vato, how does it feel?

ADAN: Powerful.

EVA: It's a bomb!

MATON: Ahora sí, now you sabe. *(Grabbing him by the hand.)* Come on, we have a lot of catching up to do! *(They both exit.)*

EVA: Adam, where are you going? Wait a minute. Wait! *(Eva walks over to the crucifix, which is all that is left of God on earth.)* Oh, my God! What are we going to do? We're going to lose all of this and be poor again, just like our parents! It isn't fair, it isn't fair! We worked so hard!

SERPIENTE: *(Entering, dressed as a priest.)* Poor Eva, she has no one to talk to, tsk, tsk. It's rather difficult to pray to a plastic Jesus, ¿que no? Mejor para mí. Excuse me won't you? I must minister to the needs of my flock. *(Crossing to Eva.)*

EVA: *(Kneeling as though at a confessional.)* Padre, Padre Ladrón?

PADRE LADRON: Yes dear, I hear you, loud and clear.

EVA: Padre, I am worried about some of the men Adam is keeping company with. He stays out all night at what they call "rap sessions." During the day he attends rallies and demonstrations in the street.

PADRE LADRON: If only men concerned themselves with spiritual matters instead of delving into politics, they would be infinitely happier.

EVA: They speak of wanting to bring down the state by any means necessary.

PADRE LADRON: Such militant rhetoric! Eve, has Adam turned into a communist?

EVA: He speaks of the poor overthrowing the rich and creating a just society.

PADRE LADRON: I thought so! Communists are the Anti-Christ! And the forces of Lucifer are marshaling like a heinous whirlwind under the red banner of socialism. Adam is associating with the Anti-Christ!

EVA: My God, he even keeps a gun in the house now . . . ever since he took up with Matón!

PADRE LADRON: My vow of silence forbids me to speak out, but if I were you I'd call the police. The phone number is PO-51313, ask for Sgt. Taco of the Red Squad.

EVA: He feels frustrated because he lost his job at the brokerage firm where he worked.

PADRE LADRON: That's right, and you're also in danger of losing your house. You are six months behind on your payments.

EVA: How did you know that?

PADRE LADRON: We hold the note on your house. The Church owns a lot of land. We need monies to carry on God's mission. Now then, anything else bothering you, be it spiritual or physical?

EVA: No. Father, is there anything you can do to help us?

PADRE LADRON: Yes, have you and Adam talked about your life in the hereafter?

EVA: What are you talking about?

PADRE LADRON: A burial plot. You see, you've got to get your reservations in early! After all, don't you want to be laid to rest in consecrated grounds tended for perpetual care?

EVA: I don't want to talk about no burial plot! I want to talk about how we're going to save our house.

PADRE LADRON: Pray, Eve, pray. Meanwhile, I'll have the boys in advertising send you some brochures through the mail. I think the plot is only $130 per month for the rest of your life. Anything else? Any deviant sexual behavior or feelings of abnormal lust?

EVA: Why are you asking me this?

PADRE LADRON: (Moving closer to her.) Why Eva, you've got to catch these practices in the bud . . . otherwise, your sex organs fall off! (Trying to fondle Eva.)

EVA: Father!

PADRE LADRON: I know about all these things, believe me!

EVA: I don't know why I bother to come to this church! Why are there no women priests?

PADRE LADRON: Shhhhh! Calm down, I was only kidding. Now then, that'll be five Hail Marys and ten Our Fathers. Don't forget Bingo on Thursdays and our special Menudo breakfast for those with hangovers on Sunday! Amen!

EVA: That did it! I'm not ever coming back here again. What a fool I've been supporting the church for all these years! (Eva exits.)

PADRE LADRON: Well, go somewhere else, join a satanic cult!

DIOS: (Appearing from up high.) ¡Diablo miserable!

SERPIENTE: Huh? Did someone say something?

DIOS: You are making a mockery of my church!

SERPIENTE: I thought you had turned into a plastic Jesus.

DIOS: I'm going to show you what a plastic Jesus I am after I wring your neck! You are perverting my flock! (Goes after Serpiente.)

SERPIENTE: ¡Ay! As if the church was so saintly. Remember, in Roma the Papas used to castrate the choirboys so they would always sing in alto.

DIOS: ¡Vicioso! ¡Odioso! (Chasing Serpiente around the stage.)

SERPIENTE: ¡Cuando en Roma, a la Romana! (As Dios grabs him.) Ay, ay, beat me, flagellate me, I love it!

DIOS: I thought I locked you up in Hell.

SERPIENTE: (Rips off his robes and escapes, faces Dios in his underwear.) And just where do you think you are anyway? Look around you . . . see the greed glowing red in the urban night? Smell the sulphurous air, the running sewers? Don't you see the corruption, can't you feel the hate? This is my Kingdom!

DIOS: Can this be true? Have I been blind all these years? What has happened to my church? What has happened to my people? I must do something, I must show myself. (The Serpiente has taken this opportunity to slip away. The light fades slowly down on Dios.)

EVA: (On another part of the stage. Enter Adán dressed as an Aztec prince.) Adam, where have you been? Just look at you, you're practically half naked. What's all this?

ADAN: Don't you see? I'm re-creating the footsteps of our indigenous forefathers. Deep down inside, this is what we really are: Aztecas!

EVA: Oh, Adam, stop living in the past!

ADAN: My name is not Adam anymore, it's Mexatexa!

EVA: Mexatexa?

ADAN: That's right, and take off that silly blonde wig! (*He rips off her wig.*)

EVA: Do you like me better as a brunette?

ADAN: I like you better as a Chicana!

EVA: Oh Adán, I love you! (*They hug.*) Darling, tell me what's wrong, you look like you haven't slept for days.

ADAN: I have been at a peyote ceremony with my Native American brothers. I had to release my gabacho/gachupín self and show the real me: ¡Azteca hasta las cachas!

EVA: (*Taking his feathers away.*) Adán, take off those feathers! You're not Aztec, your family is Yaqui from Sonora.

ADAN: The trouble with you is that (*Slightly hurt.*) you don't take the Movimiento seriously. (*He starts to leave.*)

EVA: Now, where are you going?

ADAN: To a sacrifice!

EVA: Whose sacrifice? Not yours!

ADAN: No, a gabacho's. The first Gringo we find . . . we're going to sacrifice him to the Gods.

EVA: Adán, wait, you can't do that! (*Exit Adán.*) Oh my God!

DIOS: Hello, Eva. (*Entering from the side.*)

EVA: Who are you?

DIOS: Soy Padre Cleofas, the new parish priest.

EVA: What happened to Padre Ladrón?

DIOS: Let's just say he was replaced.

EVA: It's about time, he was a no good sin vergüenza. He cared more about the collection plate than he did about our problems.

DIOS: We try to follow Jesus' example by chasing the moneylenders out of the temple.

EVA: He did do that, didn't He?

DIOS: Yes, He was in truth a humble man, a carpenter, who sided with the poor against the rich and powerful.

EVA: You know, carpenters make a pretty good living. Do you think Jesus was from the middle class?

DIOS: Ha! I never thought about that. Could be . . .

EVA: My husband and I, we had something until he lost his job. Then we lost our house.

DIOS: I hope you get everything back that rightfully belongs to you, Eva. The New Church has made a commitment to help those who need it the most.

EVA: Huh, but you don't get involved in politics, I bet.

DIOS: The Church has always been involved in politics. Christ

himself was involved in politics and that is why he was crucified
. . . for giving the common people something called "hope."

EVA: Hope in the Hereafter?

DIOS: Hope in the Hereafter and in the now. The New Church
believes that the Kingdom of Heaven should also be on Earth.

EVA: Say, where has this New Church been? I haven't heard about
it.

DIOS: It's spreading all over Latin America, Eva. The church had to
wake up to the fact that it was losing its flock. You see, it was the
shepherds who had gone astray.

EVA: Padre, how do you feel about the question of violence? You
know, as a reaction to oppression?

DIOS: Why do you ask me that, Eva?

EVA: Because Adán says he's going to kill a Gringo, tonight!

DIOS: I hope he doesn't make a big mistake.

EVA: Please, go talk to him, maybe you can help him!

DIOS: He's at the Cantina, pistiando, ¿verdad? (Blackout.)

ADAN: (Lights up at the cantina.)
> What will I do tonight
> Kill a redneck pig
> Snuff out his brief life
> Like a candle in the dark
> With the quick shot through the heart
> I'm mad and man enough to do it
> And by the devil, I'll go through it.
> But what did Eva say
> Before I left today

EVA: (Offstage.)
> If you need help sometime
> Call for the Lord Divine
> Call out his sweet name, now
> Ask him to remain, now
> He will never fail you
> Once you call he'll save you

ADAN:
> Yet there is this doubt
> My comrades wait about
> Their fingers pointed at me
> The triggers cocked and ready
> One squeeze and all is bloody
> We murder men tonight

(Muerte appears to Adán.) Who . . . are you?

MUERTE: I am La Muerte. You called for me.

ADAN: Yes, come with me tonight! I'll kill a redneck pig!

MUERTE: Wonderful! I am at your service. I guarantee my work one thousand percent and I am well-versed in hangings, stabbings, garrotings, dismemberings, poisonings, etc. We also have a special sale on burnings, malnutrition, rat bites and rapes! (*Taking Adán's hand.*)

ADAN: Death will stalk the streets
A phantom dim with stealth
When we find our target
We'll lure them into a trap
And tie them up with snakes
And feed them to the rats

MUERTE: Death will stalk the streets
Like a phantom dim with stealth
It steals into the heart
And devours it like a fruit
Soon men will be dead
They'll rot from desolation
There is no care in hatred
Only the revulsion of a soul
Turning putrid . . .

ADAN: Ay Muerte, you have sent a cold shiver up my spine!

MUERTE: Don't worry, where you're going, it's plenty warm! Ha! Ha!

ADAN: Wait a minute . . . I don't want to go through with this!

MUERTE: What? It's too late now. I'm sorry. Once you've signed the contract, there's no turning back. Besides, you're a macho, this is a macho revolution!

ADAN: No! Noooooooooo!

MUERTE: (*Pulling out a knife.*) Now then, let's get down to business. How do you want it? With a knife? (*Pulls out gun.*) Or with a gun? Or would you rather bomb them? Or take them down to the cellar, all tied up, and open up their bodies a little at a time to show them how fierce and savage I can be! Anything you want! We can even rip their hearts out and drink their steaming blood!

ADAN: Muerte, leave me be!
My God, is this really me?
I've everything to lose;
Help me, help me choose!

DIOS: (*Dios deflects Muerte's arm just as Muerte fires a shot at Adán's head.)* Adán!

ADAN: Thank God!

DIOS: The moment you even think about killing a man, you are as good as dead yourself.

MUERTE: Christian! You have thwarted me once too often!

ADAN: Watch out, Dios, he's got another gun. Look he's turned into a rinche!

DIOS: I promise you, justice *will* prevail.

MUERTE: *(Suddenly becoming a Texas ranger.)* And I'm the only justice around here. So, get outa my way, I'm just doing my job. *(Slapping Dios on the cheek.)*

ADAN: Dios! Don't let him do it!

MUERTE: You stupid Meskin! *(Trying to slap Dios again.)* Don't you know your place?

DIOS: *(Hitting La Serpiente in the face.)* Did you think I was going to turn the other cheek?

SERPIENTE: Ahhhhhhhhhh! No fair! You're supposed to be non-violent!

DIOS: You can turn the cheek once, but twice is too much!

SERPIENTE: You bloodied my nose! You bloodied my nose!

DIOS: Look, here comes Eva to help you in your struggle.

EVA: *(Entering with the standard of La Virgen de Guadalupe.)* Mira, Adán, with the Virgin de Guadalupe on our side, we can do anything. We're going to organize, register to vote and elect our own public officials. ¡Que Viva La Huelga! ¡Que Viva La Unión!

ALL: ¡Que Viva! ¡Que Viva La Raza! ¡Que Viva!

ADAN: But what if they don't let us do it peacefully, what if they keep shooting us down like dogs?

DIOS: *(Handing him a gun.)* Then keep this gun, just in case. The people have the right to defend themselves against institutionalized violence.

EVA: But let's try it my way first?

ADAN: All right. But I'll only turn the cheek once. *(All embrace and exit, except for Dios and Serpiente.)*

DIOS: So ends this scene of El Jardín
          A Chicano version of the Fall of Man
          This mixed breed of New World people
          Indian, Spanish, Negro
          Are seeing visions of their own
          Which will someday melt with the dreams of others
          To form a truly Cosmic Race *(Turning to leave.)*

SERPIENTE: (*Who has been sulking in a corner.*) Hey, not yet, there's still more to talk about.

DIOS: With you? About what?

SERPIENTE: About the dialogue between God and the Devil. Why am I always the fall guy? I have a heart. I cry, sing, bleed and feel the pangs of love. Look, wouldn't you rather live in peace?

DIOS: But of course.

SERPIENTE: Then, why don't you give me another chance?

DIOS: I don't know . . . I don't trust you.

SERPIENTE: I'll try to be more humble. I won't make so much noise. Please? I'm sick to death of my job. It's nothing but torment.

DIOS: Huh, perhaps we can arrange a minor position for you in Purgatory . . . (*Dios and Serpiente walk off conversing.*)